Metamorphosis

Echoes of Poetic Vignettes

By EmCee Kown

First Page Publications
Livonia • Michigan • USA
www.firstpagepublications.com

Cover designed by Kimberly Franzen
Illustrations by Sarah Hart

Metamorphosis / Echoes of Poetic Vignettes
EmCee Kown, 1929-
ISBN 1-928623-10-7

A life's worth of poetry in classical forms.

Library of Congress Control Number: 2004099670

First Page Publications
12103 Merriman • Livonia • MI • 48150
1-800-343-3034 • Fax 734-525-4420
www.firstpagepublications.com

Dedicated to

my beloved departed parents,
Emily E. (Crippen) and John H. McKown,

my brothers Bill and Ron,
my late husband, Everett Cleek,

my dear friend and fellow poet, Kay E. Johnson,
and a host of some very special
childhood / school friends—

Billie Ann Merry (Cherokee, Iowa), Joyce W.,
Barbara F., Iva Jeanette M., Ruth L., Myrtle K., Velma W.,
Mary H., and Jackie S. (Medical Lake, Washington)
and Paula S. of western Washington.

Author's Statement

May those who read my poetic legacy share the history, the humor, the wonders of Nature, the personality tributes, and feel the emotions they depict—and receive the joy and inspiration felt when I released the words from my heart.

In putting together this book of selected poems, I have endeavored to explore the varied forms of poetry and verse. Included are Sonnets, (for the most part, Italian style), Lyric / Rhyme, Blank and Free Verse, French Ballade, Japanese Haiku, Avant-Garde, Satire—and maybe even one or two that I created myself.

I have interjected some of my earlier efforts which date back into the mid-40s. At that time, a lot of my composition was directed towards songs—and my poetry was not as polished or governed as my current style. Some of them may, therefore, appear cumbersome, but I am including them as they are part of my poetic history.

Perhaps part of my poetry could be looked upon as controversial—and some subjects considered abrasive—but I tried to portray them delicately, or with an open mind. I leave a lot of my works to conjecture. However, my opinions are my own in the greater sense.

I have drawn upon a good many facets of life—fact, fiction, fantasy, current events, personality tributes, inspirational thoughts and ideas, speculation, etc. Things of Nature are a special favorite of mine; I find that I can expand in many directions, so they play a major role in the scope of my poems.

I have experience—hoped for—or dreamed of—many of these moods, emotions, or events—and I have tried to share them with you.

It is my sincere desire to not only entertain you, but to enlighten each of you—not only of my interpretation of Life as I see it, but of the complexities with which I have coped and dealt during my life.

Please read on on and enjoy the humor, wit, scenic wonders, love of Life and people, the beauty which can be found in even the simplest of matter—yes, even tragedy.

Poetically yours,

EmLee Kowen

My Legacy

I have no heir apparent,
No child to bear my name;
Beyond this life no bloodline
For obscurity or fame.
I do not wear a medal
As I was never brave;
But let me leave some token,
A lasting gift to save.
I have no wealth or riches,
Yet, will provides a way;
The treasures I bequeath you
Shall thrive beyond today.
May words inscribed on paper
Become my residue;
The world then be my witness
That I have journeyed through.

Ballade of a Southwest Desert

Hot vapor trails escape the sand
As Sol assaults in constant blaze
And vultures soar with contraband.
Saguaros grope in saintly praise
While desert flowers bloom in maize,
Profusely adding colour bright;
Their fragrance girds the scene like leis...
But deadly silent is the night.

The monsoon onslaught saps the land,
Eroding sage, mesquite displays.
Poor Mother Nature needs a hand
Through this destructive, savage phase
But laws of man no one obeys.
The cactus wrens in haste take flight
From predators incensed to craze...
But deadly silent is the night.

This barren region holds its stand
Where javelina mate and graze,
And rattlesnakes may leave their brand
On those encroaching, careless strays.
Adobe surface zephyr flays —
Dust devils chase and swirl with might
And thermal glares succumb to haze...
But deadly silent is the night.

The Prince of Darkness claims the rays,
Imprisoned deep within for spite
To parch and bake the caustic clays...
But deadly silent is the night.

Seasons

Spring springs and Fall falls
Summer marches in parade,
Winter beats the drum.

In The Beginning . . .

Lord, you made a beautiful World
And what I see in a lifetime is likened
To a grain of sand on an endless beach.
Let me languish in the nectar of your sweet love,
Be nourished by the ever presence of your spirit.
The wonder of life is reflected in your creation
And radiated by the heavens of your domain.
May I do justice to the time I am allotted
And leave a legacy to those who follow —
A small point of light to give guidance
Through the Eden of your Paradise, oh God,
… until the end.

False Love

The art of loving
Emanates from the brush of
A master feinter.

Gracious Lady

Stately woman, full of grace,
God has looked upon your face.
Pure and simple supplication
Shines forth in your dedication,
… Gracious Lady.
Wedded to your faith in God,
In footsteps of the Master trod.
Upon your hand His ring of gold
Pledged ever to His truths uphold,
… Gracious Lady.
Morning rounds and voice in prayer,
So God's blessings others share.
On through the day your duties gain
With saintly perseverance reign,
… Gracious Lady.
But when this life on earth is o'er
And world demands to face no more,
With grace you'll cross the great fjord
To claim your justly earned reward,
… Gracious Lady.

Sister Peter Claver, Administrator
Sacred Heart Medical Center, Spokane, WA.

The Quest

Life is relentless
In constant pursuit of death,
There is no winner.

Reverie

The faded dreams of yesterday
haunt the memory;
Tomorrow's precious hope grows faint,
synonymous to the
Veiled visions entrapped in the haze
of Indian Summer.
In the mind's eye, the fleeting images
float aloft and dim,
Likened to the trailing smoke of
burning autumn leaves.
Ethereal clouds drift and dissipate
into nothingness;
And the spirit mystique lattices the
arabesque of life,
Then frees the breath forever when the
soul is loosed at death.

The Washouts

Once deeply in love,
While airing dirty laundry,
End up with split sheets.

Fantasy

Fantasy can lure the heart
Of an unsuspecting soul
To mesmerize the thoughts and mind
So you find you lose control.
It changes daytime into night,
Even sadness into glee,

Possessing all your wakeful hours
And then steals your sanity.
Reality will soon grow dim,
You are drawn out from its realm;
For if you dream away too long
An addiction takes the helm.
Our dreams are only fleeting things
Not meant to last forever,
Go rid yourself of reverie
And face your life endeavor.
Come back, come back, oh, captive one
Before it becomes too late;
Accept the truths the future holds
You cannot alter your fate.
The fact is you should live your life
The way it was meant to be,
Instead of being bound in chains
By your wasted fantasy.

Anthem to America

With bosoms bared to greet the newborn day
And tasseled vegetation girding loins,
The rivers flow from your directive quoins
To freshen verdant patchwork set inlay.
While oceans lap your shores of mottled clay,
The Great Divide astrides with mighty groins
To separate the slope whence East-West joins
And Mankind finds a temple where to pray.

Anatomy of all the elements
Contained within your earthen body shell
Might be the seminal of innocence.
The peace and refuge of your citadel,
Begotten by the strength of opulence,
Forever may the winds of war you quell.

Bon Voyage

Upon the Sea of Life the frigates sail,
These lardered vessels in their earthly garb;
Preparing for the battle of travail,
With spirits high they bait the angler's barb.
As fishermen of men, they toss their nets
To draw the weary traveler to port;
A haven in a storm, atoning debts,
With praise they glide in grace, all ilk and sort.
When bread upon the waters shall be cast,
Rewards are garnered in that Godly realm;
And souls transported from their worldly past
Are ransomed by the Master at the helm.

The Saga of the Soaps

The COAST was clear and so he thought
He'd DIAL her on the phone
To tell her all the CHEER she brought,
But couldn't get a TONE.
A SWEETHEART of a gal was she,
So bet for all your LIFEBOY,
The TREND of dreams he hoped would be
Should bring him lots of JOY!
He longed to SHIELD her in his arms,
CARESS her IVORY skin — but
To DASH the race he needed charms
To turn the TIDE and win.
So SNUGGLE closely until DAWN,
Be BOLD with words of love;
Upon the SURF drift like a swan,
Coo like a turtleDOVE.
For SAFEGUARD dares he not to SHOUT,
His tears CASCADE the house.
A CINCH his lady love, no doubt,
Will never LEVER spouse.

Though and When

Though we are total strangers,
we know each other well.
Though we have never touched,
we feel the same emotions.

Though we have never talked,
we converse in many ways.
Though miles may separate us,
we ever near remain.
When happiness engulfs you,
it radiates to me.
When joy you spread,
it makes my spirits soar.
When you are melancholy,
the pensiveness enshrouds me.
When pain persists,
I ache to ease your hurts.
Though foreign to each other,
we walk on common ground.
Though speak we different tongues,
we share a global language.
When poets put their pens to paper,
the world is in their hands.
When the eyes perceive the written word,
our hearts and souls are one.

True Beauty

The saying that beauty is only skin deep
To some may well apply.
The hint of a smile, a sensuous voice,
The flirtatious twinkling eye.
The beauty as seen by the passers by
Sow seeds which misrepresent,
Flaunting itself to the eyes of the world,
Reaping a gross discontent.
The beauty of flesh will fade as a rose,
Leaving behind a false pride;
Masking the beauty which once shown forth,
With nature you now must abide.
But beauty to God, your home and your friends,
So rewarding is its goal,
For beauty, true beauty, comes from within
Divining the heart and the soul.

An Old Fashioned Thanksgiving

As summer fades into winter
And the harvested fields are all bare,
There's a day set aside for Thanksgiving

Of sincere supplication and prayer.
To those who have long gone before us,
'Twas not just a day set for feast,
But instead it was hallow'd and sacred
To give thanks for the toils that had ceased.
With prayerful hearts they were gathered
On that initial Thanksgiving Day;
They were true and sincere in their worship
In the typical old-fashioned way.
Redman and White grouped together,
In peace and contentment they stood,
While on tables made ready before them
Was the seasoned and well-garnished food.
Tradition has added more splendour
And custom has taken its place,
But thanksgiving that comes from the heart
Is something you cannot erase.
Through the hills now echo the memories
Of the time whence the settlers first trod,
Seeking an old fashioned Thanksgiving
With simple, true worship of God.

Blind Justice

When the verdict was rendered,
The world reeled in disbelief.
Were we deceived by what our eyes beheld?
Giving vent to the emotions of the outcome,
Tempers flared and neighborhoods were
Ripped apart with deadly force.
Though betrayed by the system, a small, meek voice
Called upon the multitude to cease the violence.
"can we get along, can we get along?
We must stop for there are people who
Will never go home — it isn't right,
Let's try to work it out!"
Like the uneasy calm that follows a hurricane,
Cautiously, they venture out into the devastation.
Cast your eyes skyward, look up, the scales
Weigh heavy, but allow love to overcome all;
Justice shall, ultimately, prevail!

Rodney King

Three Ships

They sail away those vessels up on high,
Flotilla floats of beauty in the sky;
And voyage on to far-off foreign lands
Or take a brief sojourn as need demands.
Celestial hordes play games of hide and seek
Above the fruited plain or mountain peak;
They thrill to ride the waves of windswept crests
Or pause to touch, caress the earthly breasts.
The desert ships are languid, down to earth,
Indifferent to a milieu mundane birth;
Their canter like the rolling ocean swells,
Among the dunes the dromedary dwells.
Content with rudimental, landlocked lives,
This blatant beast of burden lowly thrives;
In caravans the camels cruise the sand
With skippers who are chasing contraband.
Recall the pioneers of yesteryear
Who drift from East to West in constant fear;
To quell the wilderness of the unknown,
They didn't have to sail their ship alone.
Their faithful prairie schooner brought the brave
Undaunted ones across the grassy wave;
These emigrants set course on lifelong dreams
Upon the tempest Sea of Life, it seems.
With hands of Fate on helm, the craft drifts free
To face the things of life that are to be;
The buoyant hopes of those who self-embark
Reflect upon the deeds that leave their mark.
As different as is shown their style or mode,
However you may seek your own abode;
Be it clouds or beast or wagon that sets sail,
You master your own ship, succeed or fail!

Dactyl Love

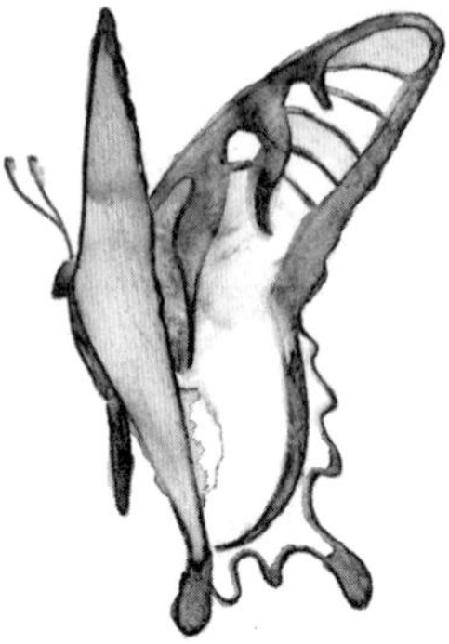

Love is elusive in so many ways,
But yet the foundation of life.
Facets reflect the emotions in depth,
At peace with oneself or in strife.
Love is a colour, a rainbow's delight,
So varied in shades and in hues;
Soft pastel pinks into bright cherry reds
To darkest and deepest of blues.
Love is vivacious, precocious and bold,
Or calm as a vast mirrored sea;
Hold it with tenderness, sharing your lot,
But let not yourself possessed be.
Love is alive to be nurtured with care,
Just prune it as you cultivate;
Handle with kindness and don't lose control
As love should not rule, dominate.
Life is the blessed outpouring of love
Which God bestowed first upon Man;
Hope for tomorrow is promised today
For life beyond this meager span.

You Can't Go Back

So many years have passed since the childhood
days of yore —
I recall the host of friends there used to be;
The elements of time have erased or
dimmed the view,
Yet recollections stir my memory.
Box elder trees abound when the tulips
are in bloom,
A scent of goldenrod is in the air;
The tiny creek which flooded is curling
through the fields,
And wrens have built their nests in sylvan hair.
The thoughts I can associate with times of
growing up;
We chased the fireflies on a summer's eve;
Made queenly dolls of hollyhocks, wore
dandelion rings —
We lived a simple life, as you perceive.
On sidewalks we played hopscotch, rollerskated
or jumped rope,

Awakened to the peaceful cooing dove;
In Springtime we sought Mayflowers, then walnuts
in the Fall,
And Sunday dinners shared with those we love.
They tell me things are different now and most my
friends are gone —
A freeway splits the north side from the south;
The creek has been diverted and a super
market thrives,
But news still travels best by word of mouth.
You can't slow down the clock or reverse the
hands of time,
Now neighborhoods, familiar landmarks lack;
And labors of the journey that you take are
all for naught,
'Tis said, and aptly so, "You can't go back!"

Serenade

The glow of twilight spreads its golden wings,
And dusk o'er takes the glimmer of the day
As shadows flit and flicker in ballet.
The vesper music in the gloaming brings
A gentle zephyr breeze which softly sings
Its melody of Nature's grand soiree.
While crickets chirp their pensive roundelay,
The wafted choral harmony enclings.

A mocking bird then trills a lullaby
At midnight just to soothe the nestling brood.
With praise and laud the sounds then amplify,
Embellishing the orchestrated mood.
The realm of Phoebus stirs within the sky,
An advent overture to Dawn's prelude.

Scavengers

There are those who may rummage through daydreams
In search of a memory or two,
Or they sweep out the past in their forage
With hopes they can salvage a few.
As they pilfer the days that are bygone
In quest for some sweet reverie,

The scraps that they find are reminders
Of things which you no longer see.
While the remnants of life are encaptive
In minds that are dimmed now with years,
Still the heart has the key to the treasures
Of souls that the faithful reveres.
Being born with a spoon that is silver
May endow them with ancestral wealth;
Yet the most cherished largess to pray for
Are the blessings bestowed by good health.

Jewels

Life is like a strand of pearls
Strung in random lengths.
Quality, not quantity or size, is
The measure of value.
The radiance created may reflect
Diamond prisms, or be
Absorbed within the murky depths
Of the mysterious opal.
Life may spark the glow of topaz,
Or the clarity of the ruby...
Be as pied as the agate or as
Lustrous as the sapphire.
From lowly beginnings, the earthly
Gems you are may earn a
Lofty mounted throne illuminated by
The jewels in your saintly crown.

Close Encounter

Two hearts passed in the dark of night
And brushed against arms of love;
Unspent emotions stirred up inside
Take flight as wings of a dove.
Like empty hulls adrift on the sea
Be it duty or desire?
Questions unspoken, ever aglow,

Kindle a decadent fire.
Forbidden thoughts and fantasies
Lured by a haven of hope;
Reach they out in wild desperation
For happiness — blindly grope.
The voyage beyond cannot be launched,
It is bound by fate to fail;
Abandon the ship or change the course,
Drop anchor in lieu of sail!
Hold dear the hopes, the desires, the dreams;
For Destiny maps the charts;
A close encounter may not come true,
This journey set by two hearts.

The Thaw

Sol warms the season,
Snowdrifts weep their lives away
And melt into Spring.

Michael's Gone

Lost in the deafening silence is his boyish chuckle,
The memory of his impish grin.
Absent is the mischievous twinkle in his eyes,
The softened gaze of compassion and understanding.
The tousled hair that haloed his head
Went by the ways of the wind.
The miracle he prayed for could not be; this island
Of brilliance is set adrift from the mainland.
He shall be sorely missed; his earthly sojourn
Left a host of friends who love him dearly —
Not for what he was — but what he inspired them to be.
The legacy lives on in the joys bestowed upon others.
His star shines brightly on a higher plain —
Aloft to grace a new wilderness adventure.
Methinks the world is just a little better place
Because Michael paused awhile as he passed through.

Michael Landon
(Little House on the Prairie) (Highway to Heaven) (Bonanza)

Butterflies

Multi beauties waft
On psychedelic wings like
Stained glass in the sky.

Romance of the Seasons

There is beauty in every season
From Winter on through Fall,
But the beauty found in Springtime
Has captivated all.
For it's then that love comes courting
With a fragrance all its own,
Entwining hearts of lovers
And puts them on a throne.
So, on into Summer drifts romance
With depthening brightness of hue,
Flaunting the richness of colours and
Wishing for dreams to come true.
But, when Summer fades into Autumn
Some darkening shadows appear,
While the broken-hearted lovers
Are harvesting sorrows and tears.
And now we see Winter approaching
Complete with its bleakness and pain,
Yet, will the slumbering heart awaken
To welcome the Springtime again?

Saint Helens

In May of eighty,
The retching crater coughs and
Vomits its contents.

Friends

A friend you were
A friend, indeed;
You came to cheer
This friend in need.
You always left
The day more bright;
So many things
Once wrong, now right.
'Twas pre-determined
At the start;
We could not share
Each other's heart.
You set the limits
Then crossed them, too;
Desires you showed,
So, lines I drew.
The friendship grew
Perhaps too fast;
Then took a turn
Which could not last.
Although 'twas never
Meant to be
You soon were more
Than friend to me.
Two lonely hearts
Reached out to pray;
But too much romance
Got in the way.
You may have felt
The same soft tug;
Arousing needs
Each time we'd hug.
Soft kisses then
Demanded more
Than we, as friends,
Had bargained for.
Just where it ends
I do not know;
But friendships true
Need room to grow.
I thank my God
For the friend you be,
And the part of life
You shared with me!

Love Games

The contract rules in the game called love,
You take the hand that fate deals;
So, bid for hearts as you wait on deck,
Or pass up tricks it reveals.
Don't raise the bet, bridge the run, play straight,
Just meld or draw to a flush;
It gives a chance to renege or fold,
Spade discards under, don't blush.
Go join the club, shoot the moon on high,
Or pair with diamonds bright;
A marriage now and a full house then,
Keep score and play your cards right!

The Eagle Screams

A symbol of might this awesome bird of prey
Circling, ever circling in the sky,
Watchful of the hordes with eager eye.
Be they subjects or victims, who's to say?
Who will survive and who will pass away?
Perched aloft with powerful wings to fly
And pluck the unsuspecting souls to die
From a predator we tribute pay.

Righteous? Ruthless? Intellects command,
"Appease the appetite, let talons lash,
Feed and satiate carnivorous stand."
When finished, all will mourn and teeth will gnash.
Aggregate the populous of Promised Land,
Let History reflect the mortal clash.

Hark, The Mocking Bird Doth Sing

As Nature's reveille awakes the Morn,
Auroral fingers probe the darkened skies
With light of Dawn, a virgin day is born.
'Tis time for all Mankind to stir and rise
And softly, as the shadows start to fade,
A chortled happy sound wafts through the rays
To herald the advent birth, it lifts the shade

So all the World may take and offer praise.
... Hark, the mocking bird doth sing!

The midday sun climbs high within its realm,
A harbinger astride a vast expanse.
Remains it steady, master at the helm,
But coursing downward leaving naught to chance.
The Daybreak metamorphosis seeks Dusk,
Explores the azure sea with cloudy fleet,
While twilight folds her drapes, the day grows brusque,
From deep within its throat the notes entreat.
... Hark, the mocking bird doth sing!

The solar sojourn yields to evening tide
As cooling zephyrs freshen all at hand.
With curtains drawn the groom awaits his bride,
And lunar disc traverses o'er the land.
While moonbeams guide the way throughout the dark,
The velvet night is polka dot with stars.
Then, once again the vesper songs embark
So like a host of symphony guitars.
... Hark, the mocking bird doth sing!

Innocence

The world with all its complex doubts
Could well afford to heed
A meek solution simplified
To solve an age-old need.
For peace and full tranquility
Which knows no segregation,
Embrace your foreign countrymen
And strengthen multi-nation.
Accept in faith your fellow man
Question not intent or goal
By color, faith, his race or creed,
Be it East, or West, or Pole.
The answers from the mouths of babes,
Sincere from every sibling,
Ignoring prejudice of life
Knows neither pauper nor king.
The innocence portrayed by youth
Reflects trust undefiled,
With the mirrored admiration
Through the eyes of mundane child.

The Cry of a Broken Heart

Some say it is better to have loved and lost
Than to never have loved at all,
But ofttimes the ache of a broken heart
Makes you wish you couldn't recall.
There are times, and places and things of the past
All relics of a dead romance;
The joys and bliss for which you once dreamed
But was never given a chance.
'Twas only a blossom on a field of gray —
A flower which faded and died,
And with it all hope for happiness,
In its stead, a love long denied.
So, don't be fooled by words such as these,
"Tis better to have loved and lost,"
For it's those who loved and ultimately won
That know not the grief and its cost.

A Gathering of Crows

There they are — lined up on the rail
or strutting about just out of reach.
Watching, ever watching, with the glut
of a thousand vultures,
Their evil darkness intensifies as the
shadows of Dusk draweth nigh.
The orts of Man, consumed by the
ravenous demons of Life,
Become the skeletal remains of
what used to be...
Dead, but yet alive — rejuvenated
by the Dove of Dawn
Which stretches forth her wings
to embrace the battered Soul.

Hope of Dawn

Dawn is stirring in the East
Stretching forth fingers of light,
Waking the soul of the universe
From the velvet dark of night.

Like pinnacles of radiant gold
The rays come showering down
To paint the sphere in iris hues,
And adorn it as a crown.
All Nature seems to sense new life
Reborn in heavens clear;
It trembles and arouses from
A restless night of fear.
A pausing world looks on in awe,
Then bursts forth into song,
And welcomes back to human realm
This dawn of hope — the hope of Dawn.

Fair Weather Friends

The need was great, but where were you,
My countless friends of yore?
I lent you many precious hours,
Support I did implore.
When judgment errors came to pass,
A few stood at my side;
But others turned their backs to me,
There was no place to hide.
The faithful voiced encouragement
And eased my aching heart,
While bigots bathed in self-esteem,
No comfort to impart.
The hype exploited by the mass,
"Sensation" stroked their pen;
They cared not for the captive soul
Imprisoned deep within.
The prayers and kindly acts of love
Came from a loyal few;
But shattered trust encompassed me,
I searched, but where were you?

The King and Di

Innate trait puts a
Royal marriage on the rocks;
Crowns make not a King.

Fireplace

Fireplace with your flaming lights,
Comfort brings on wintry nights.
Patterns deepen in the glow,
Feats of magic steal the show.
Coals grow nervous, discontent,
Jump until their spark is spent.
Shadows flicker on the wall,
As the fire tides rise and fall.
Embers cool upon their bed,
While their smoky tears are shed.
All life faces compromise,
Logs char to their own demise.
Princely flames grimace in pain,
Only ashes now remain.

Anita

Rocks she gently in the chair — her
mind uncluttered by the evils
and worries of life.
With joyful thoughts and trusting eyes
she finds happiness in the solitude
of her innocent being.
Freely, she gives her love and demands a
just return — realizing not that
she's a gifted one.
She extends a hand and seeks the
comfort of guidance while suspended
in a mental time warp.
Remains she ever captive in her
own private world, this
benign, eternal child.

Anita Cleek (1944–2000)

The Gallant Seven

Awake the Dawn, prepare yourselves, oh, Fates.
Today the mysteries of life unfold
When Destiny, thus beckons to the bold,
The brave, undaunted ones, approach the Gates.
With faith each hero dares, then advocates
To challenge worlds unknown beyond the hold.
The course you set exemplifies your mold,
Tho' History may weep, you kept your dates.

Fear not, ye souls, rise up, new pathways trod.
Go forge ahead, condition and enleaven;
With courage walk, your footsteps valor shod,
Uncharted startreks pioneered in Heaven.
Forever in the bosom of your God,
Your legacy lives on, oh Gallant Seven.

Animal Antics

While LION on the beach one day
CAT-napping in the sun,
A night-MARE came from out the blue,
My HARE-brain came undone.
I stalled by playing POSSUM,
My HART was in my throat —
But using HORSE-sense I out-FOXED
The MULEY COW-ard's GOAT.
You cannot BURRO head in sand
Or RAVEN, rant and CROW,
For jail-BIRDS come from ROBIN banks
Instead of BUCKS and DOE.
The SQUIRRELY way this world is now
You dare not CHICKEN out,
Or DUCK behind a DOG-wood bush
To FAWN when you're in doubt.
'Twas more than I could really BEAR,
One OTTER know, in strife —
BULL-headedness can never win
This RAT-race known as life.

Wild Stallion

Untamed as the wind,
Nostrils flared and eyes ablaze,
Demands free spirit.

The Journey

On the ocean of life, you may float with the tide,
Like a drifter without any goal;
But beyond the horizon, just out of your view
Lies a haven which beckons your soul.
While you stand at the bow in the salt breezy spray,
Leave your cares far behind in the wake;
To the passage hold true and veer not from the course,
Put your faith in the voyage you take.
But as storm clouds engulf you, the tempest grows wild,
In the darkness you grope for your dream;
Then a hand takes the helm and it guides you ashore
While the beacon shines forth with its beam.
You see, life is a journey and destined to be
Like a sojourn with some foreign clan;
So, be true to your values and seek to attain
That perfection sought after by Man.

Bubble Bath

Bubbles float aloft
And startle the atmosphere
With bursting splatters.

Soul Search

Lord, did I hurt someone today,
Or say an unkind word?
Did I betray a confidence,
Repeat something I heard?
Did I a falsehood tell a friend —

Trespass beyond the line
To better just the ego self,
Or take what wasn't mine?
Lord, did I fall to evilness,
Become enslaved to lust?
Neglect to pay the homage due
To those who love and trust?
Should I excuse my fellow man
For something he has done?
Or beg forgiveness for myself
From Thee, oh Holy One?

Emergency Broadcast System

The fragile balance Nature holds in tow
Is being tampered with by would be gods,
Who choose, at will, those to remain or go,
Manipulating fate and playing odds.
'Tis written that these things will come to pass
When man shall gnash his teeth and quake in fear,
And there will be no solace for the mass
But brutal loss of that which we hold dear.

The luminary elements are strained
And Mankind stands upon the very brink
When molten atoms loose their wrath unchained;
The time is drawing nearer than you think.
The chilling statement, "THIS IS NOT A TEST!"
Eternal darkness gains its deadly quest.

The Window

Peering through the mist of years
At the mirrored reflection on
The far side of the window of Life,
One perceives that
The yesterdays were each
The tomorrows of the many
Todays of time gone by
. . . And the eyes are dimmed by
Trailing tears that trickle
down the pane.

Jack Frost and His Magic Brush

This time of year you feel it when
A nip is in the air,
The crops have all been harvested
And fields lay mown and bare.
When apple trees await caresses
As their cheeks they clutch,
And ripened fruit turns rosy red
From that special touch.
The pumpkins lie in readiness
To glow in colour bright,
Enhancing every childhood dream
For Halloween delight.
The maple and the aspen blaze
In variegated hue,
While leaves take on a splendour from
The crispness of the dew.
As dawn awakes, the crystal ice
Forms castles on the panes,
The phantom artist strikes again,
The season when he reigns.
A toss of this, a fling of that
Which make a maiden blush,
For Autumn bids a welcome,
Mister Jack Frost and his brush.

No Trespassing

Encroachment fishing
Lures the tall-tale sportsman by
Hook, line and sinker.

First Flight

Anticipating, there you sit
With seatbelt fastened tight,
The thrust of power is at your back,
And soon the wings take flight.
You watch the ground fade underneath

Into a patchwork world,
Your shadow skips across the quilt,
A new scene is unfurled.
In mystic mode the map below
Spreads out in activation;
The hills, like billows of a tent,
Undulate in animation.
The penciled roadways of the land
Reach out like seamstress stitches,
You watch in awe the ribbon streams
Trail through their watery ditches.
You're climbing yet, then suddenly,
The artistry grows dim
As wisps of clouds enclose your craft
And captivate the glim.
Then cresting out on top you hear
And feel the jet thrust slow;
You gaze at pillow puffs of white
Afloat in the herds below.
The piercing sunlight penetrates
Your eyes search out the view,
Vast pinnacles of mountain peaks
Display themselves to you.
The captain's voice comes clear and sharp,
"All turbulence we beat
By flying high above it all
At forty-thousand feet."
The time goes quickly by and soon
You sense the downward trend,
While knifing through the cumulus
You near your journey's end.
Beyond the rugged coastline cliffs,
The ocean sprawls beneath,
As trailing wakes of motorboats
Create a foamy wreathe.
Your pilot head the plane for shore,
You see the famous Bay.
Awestruck are those who visit there,
What more is there to say?
Upon the runway touching down,
You glow in sheer delight,
For it is a grand occasion
To experience your first flight!

The Poet

The pen strokes beauty
In multi-hues, creating
A bouquet of words.

The Master Plan

In the vastness of the Universe
Man is but a small pinnacle of light,
And the stars of the heavens are scattered
Like dotted swiss upon black velvet.
Time seems to stand still, yet
As a graceful swan, day glides into dusk.
With the delicate balance of Nature,
Dawn lifts its curtains to explode into colour,
And a symphony resounds in the skies.
Phoebus smiles from aloft.
God is good, God is great;
Come to the table and sup —
Drink and partake of His splendour.

Horizons

Just beyond the scope of vision
Looking forward — looking back,
Are the questions and the answers
To the many things we lack.
Happiness has been evasive,
Always there but out of reach;
Measure of success is worthless,
Best we practice what we preach.
Never ending is the cycle —
Health and wealth go hand in hand;
One does not beget the other
With some promised contraband.
Out of sight, not out of mind is
Not a case of seek and hide;
Things will look so very different
When you're on the other side.

Buried Treasure

The token things we hide away
And store for future pleasure
So often lose their luster glow
Which made them such a treasure.
Though precious when we hid them there,
They bordered on perfection,
But memories of that moment lost
Escape our recollection.
Perhaps a bloom from yesterday,
A dried corsage so faded
With petal crumbling in your hand,
The ribbons tied and braided.
A teardrop trickles from your eye
As letters from a loved one
Come drifting through your reverie,
Those wistful days came undone.
But life goes on and hopes don't die,
For that you should be happy;
The buried treasures you forgot
Are held within your psyche!

Ready the Gladiators

As desert storm clouds gather o'er the sand,
The day of reckoning dawns in the East
To fling the gauntlet at the glutton Beast
And shower destruction on a war-ripe land.
The Mother of all battles is at hand
While orisons implore the Advent feast
To end the tyranny of satan's priest
And free the harried victims from command.

The nations of the world hang on the brink
As portents of the times confront Mankind.
They seek the binding chains' most weakened link,
Then concentrate on breaking what they find.
The cock crowed midst the strife and out of sync;
Can Armageddon be that far behind?

The Fledglings

The nestling brood dares
To awkwardly flutter like
Passe' propellers.

Speculation

If I could but go back and reverse
the sands of time
I wonder at the changes I would make;
The many arrowed crossroads when life
was in its prime,
What altered aims that I would undertake.
Were I to take the left branch instead
of turning right,
Would I end up a victor — reach my goal?
The mainstream may be easy, but challenge
dares delight,
Rejoicing can rejuvenate the soul!
The rainbow's pot of gold may not always
be my prize,
But yet, I can't give up for just suppose,
The end is the beginning and hope
thus never dies,
The magic of the moment ever glows!
So mulling over daydreams won't change
a single thing,
And wishing cannot vary tides which flow;
Just strive to reach the stars and feel
the heart take wing,
The alternate, I guess, I'll never know!

A House Divided

Love cannot abide and thrive
In a house that's filled with hate;
A family pulled asunder
Must some day meet its fate.
With brother loathing brother
And mistrust on every turn,
Is it really any wonder
That the fires of contempt burn?
Faith is an unheard virtue
By the members of the clan,
It's a dog-eat-dog position
Down to the final man.
Any effort made to salvage
Is looked upon with scorn,
And the goat's left tethered, helpless,
Rejected and forlorn.
The nightmare is climaxing
As the hour of truth draws near;
Whether all is gained or all is lost
Depends on common peer.
The forces of the family
Perch as vultures in the gloam,
For a house that is divided
Can never be a home!

The Flood

Unrelenting rains
Falling on a thirsty world
Oversate the soil.

Tacit Travail

I wonder what my life would be had my birthright
been sustained.
Might I fly the heavens like a bird transporting
souls aloft?
Or perhaps minister to the sick and ailing,
dying clan?
Would I man or woman be . . . enriched with wealth
or fame or both?
Or a mudane farmer enhancing the balance
of Nature?
Oh, how I long for freedom from my ultimate
destiny!
I lie in wait, yearning, but they say my days
are numbered.
The choice was never mine to make, predestined
to never be.
Fragile, forlorn and unwanted, I labor in
vain for birth.

The Botanist's Nightmare

The dandelion is reigning king in yard
menageries
O'er gentle pussywillows and queenly
tiger lilies.
The snapdragons are standing guard beside a
crystal pool,
A trailing spiderwort is draped at the foot
of a toadstool.
A monkshood daily herds a flock of cowslips
out to pasture,
While a cattail lurks in waiting to pounce on
a small larkspur.
A skunk cabbage stands all alone, as does a
sour gooseberry,
And on a pond a duckweed floats while broods of
henbane tarry.
A striped zebra plant cavorts with a peppery
horseradish,
While a pigweed sates his hunger by munching in
the bulrush.
A venus flytrap waits for lunch; dogwoods bay

at the moon,
Then a foxglove joins in harmony to howl a
mournful tune.
A wolfsbane masquerades about in garbs of a
sheep sorrel,
Amongst the phlox secreted, underneath a
stalked umbel.
Though mostly borne of fantasy, this jungle
like portrayal,
Don't ever take for granted Wild Kingdom's
plant arrayal!

Beauty

Iridescent wings
Reflect rainbow colours of
The common housefly

The Rainbow of Life

A rainbow can compare to Life
With hues in diverse range,
Beginning from the day of birth,
The colours dim or change.
A glowing youth, Life winds its way
Throughout the candid years,
Where growing pains, like summer rains
Produce a shower of tears.
The prism arches to the skies
And days of teen-age plights,
Where mixed emotions cloud the minds
For maidens and their knights.
Perfection ever strives to be —
Look upward and beseech,
When time stands still and slowly wanes,
An apex, thus we reach.
As rainbows fade then so must Life,
The shades of night unfold;
Rewards found at the rainbow's end
Are lifetime pots of gold.

Carousels

Merry-go-rounds whirl
On continuous flights, and
Chase dreams forever.

Diana, Princess of Wales

Compassion was reflected on her face,
A jewel for the masses to behold;
Untarnished by the riches found in gold,
The multitudes were nourished by her grace.
With winsome smile as delicate as lace,
The fostered hopes impart abiding mold
To those who, by themselves, could not be bold,
Their lives drew strength and love from the embrace.

Though destined not for Queendom in her days,
She ruled with charm the many of command.
Her simple royalty in common ways,
Respected by the hordes, this Lady grand.
A champion for the meek that life portrays,
Her spirit reigns in hearts throughout the land.

Diana, Princess of Wales (1961–1997)

Prayer

When you are feeling lonely
    And your heart is in despair,
There's a way to consolation —
    That way you'll find is prayer.
When days are never ending
    And nights are filled with terror,
Fear not, for God is with you —
    Call out to Him in prayer.
When toils of life are heavy
    Or your mind is wrought in care,
Don't ever feel discouraged —
    Just breathe a silent prayer.
When life on earth is over
    There is happiness to share;
You can gain it all so simply —
    By seeking God in prayer.

Lake Serenity

As you gaze across the tranquil bay
Seeking out the distant crystal shore,
Fleeting wisps of fog go trailing by
To reflect a dream of yesteryore.
Tiny dewdrops hail the virgin day,
Bring refreshment to the world below;
Lake bugs skitter on the placid plain
Playing leapfrog in the solar glow.
Trout come up to kiss the sunny dawn
Searching for a tasty breakfast treat;
Down they settle then to safer depths,
The hour presents a newborn day to greet.
Babbling brooklets tumble down the banks,
Zephyr breezes waft the clouds about;
Creatures stir and stalk the native prey,
Then the muted silence seems to shout!
Shadows start to stretch their eerie arms,
Curtains drop the dusky shades of night;
Fireflies spark a message set in code,
Crickets chirp their piercing mournful plight.
Tolling chimes caress a vesper hymn,
Peacefully, they lift the spirits high;
Morpheus then dusts the eyes with sleep
As nature sings its bedtime lullaby.

Blessed Event

A new little life has been forming inside
So close to its mother's heart,
Grows daily more cherished to husband and wife,
A new generation will start.
Wanted for long by the parents to be,
The cherub whose being means much,
Anticipation beyond all their dreams
To have and to hold and to touch.
They watch and are beaming with joy and pride
As the seed of life takes on form,
Thoughts of football, baseball or fishing and such,
Or visions of "Queen of the Prom."
The heartbeat grows stronger with each passing month,
Soon movement sensations will start,

The precious one labors for that special day
    When maternal releases impart.
Baby girl, baby boy, whichever it be —
    This product of parental love,
Tender moments to plan the future ahead
    For that blessed event from above!

The Hawk and The Dove

With furtive eyes that spark of embered coals,
And tools of war clenched tightly in his claws
To wrest from those devoted to the cause —
Awaits he, vantaged high to pluck the souls
Of all who seek emancipated goals.
The meed of conquest earns its just applause
And gathers strength from advocated laws,
Intrinsic pride proclaimed by placid shoals.

Look up, beyond the forces fueled by hate —
The salient seraph Amity calls, "Cease,
Subversive evils, heed the voice of Fate;
Eject the strifeful elements!" Release
The mighty wings of love thru Earthdom's gate,
Oh, valiant victor, harbinger of Peace.

Meditation

The spores of Life
    May often be no more than fantasies forgotten
                    Or desires never fulfilled . . .
But as long as they nurture on
    The reflections of yesterday,
                    The reality of today,
                            And the dreams of tomorrow,
Hope does not die
    But continues to thrive
                    Within the psyche of one's being.

Castles in the Sand

While strolling on the beach one day and gazing
out to sea,
My mind a thousand miles away, my cares were
loose and free.
I stumbled on a mound of sand, some child had
been at play,
And as the tide edged closer, his dreams would
wash away.
I stopped and thought a moment, and pondered
at the sight;
How fragile are material things when put in
proper light.
The castle built upon the sand will crumble,
dissipate,
Be lost and gone forever, prepared not
for its fate.
Your dreams must have foundation if they are
to come true,
So nurture them with kindness and imbibe with
spirit, too.
Survival of the treasures is based on
God-sent love,
For lifetime jewels are founded in that
Kingdom up above.

The Cycle of the Icicle

Conceived by nature's act of life
From out the atmosphere,
It spikes a growth inside itself
To lengthen and adhere.
This finial of crystal ice
Along the rooftop eaves,
While captivating those below
Compounds what it receives.
Its life span, unpredictable,
Though tries it to prolong,
A hardened heart that beats within
Is said to not be strong.

An icy finger stretches forth
Aspiring to gain size;
In doing so, it sheds a tear,
And starts its own demise.
The once proud army cycle corps
Must pray for a rebirth
For sunlight tends to warm the soul
Of those who dwell on Earth.
So gracefully they melt away,
But not for long, of course;
The season only just began
And they'll be back in force!

Cobwebs

Go sweep aside the misty webs
The years with skill have spun;
The artistry of woven strands
That tinsel in the sun
The iridescent memories
That span the tides of time
Are ever present in the mind,
Life's poem set in rhyme.
A stroking brush with pastel hues
Paints portraits in the mesh,
Creating mindful reveries
To liven and refresh.
But life is short when twilight falls
And yesterdays are past;
Beyond the veil of Eden lies
Eternity, at last!

Crumbs from the Table of Life

I never had a childhood,
It was wrung from me with wrath;
The dreams of youth proved nightmares
As I crawled along the path.
The joys of going swimming,
Or of marching in a band,

With misty eyes I reached in faith,
Denied, my outstretched hand.
The dating and the dancing, and
Romantic "first kiss" blush,
Never came pulsating to me,
It was shattered by the hush.
The problems faced when growing up
Engulfed me overnight;
Awoke I in a strange new world,
Bewildered at my plight.
Forsaken by the friends I knew,
Untethered from the past;
Watching, ever waiting, but
The dye had long been cast.
To gain an education nearly
Took an act of God;
For obstacles were many as
The road of Life I trod.
The awes of youth, envisioned hopes,
Then faded and were gone —
Held captive in this ravaged shell
Of one who must go on.
Enshrouded dreams, un-nurtured, left
A mere rejected token;
One cannot feast on crumbs of life
When spirits have been broken.

May–December Romance

They dated through high school and so,
It was thought they would marry, but no;
He fell for another
Her very own mother —
And that was the end of her beau!

Autumn Tapestry

The woven strands of summer
Unravel day by day,
A new scene is unfolding
In a chain-reaction way.
The smoke clouds spiral upward
To create a muraled sky,

With patterns ever changing
    Like a fleet of ships on high.
The threads are interlacing
    In a woof and warp entwine
To floss the season's fabric
    For an intricate design.
The blushing leaves will cushion
    When a crispness fills the air,
As filtered harvest moonglow
    Beams on forest's thoroughfare.
Mother Nature, master weaver,
    Decorates the countryside
In brilliant waves of colour,
    Undulating with the tide.
The face of Earth embroidered
    By majestic artistry
Displays the painted texture
    Found in Autumn Tapestry.

Beau Brandy

He's gone . . .
His little footsteps on the floor
        click no more.
The steady snore of his nap
        is silent — gone forever.
We mourn your departure, Dear One.
Rest in peace . . .
        Our beloved Brandy sleeps.

Beau Brandy (12-3-79 to 10-19-89)

Little Pooh

Gone is the quizzical gaze as you
        search out our faces,
And the silence of your incessant
        yap is deafening.
All the companionship and love of your
        creature being is held in endearment.
We cherished you in life . . .
        we mourn you in death.
You have joined your sibling brother in
        the arms of eternal sleep,
But you live forever in our hearts.

Little Pooh (12-3-79 to 9-22-90)

Regal Sol

As Morning lifts the shades of Night
From East to West across the dome;
Old Sol begins his daily flight
Among the planets, arcing home.
Concealed in darkness, yesterday,
Tomorrow's promise lies ahead;
A brightness beams upon today
As glory 'round the world is spread.
In constant journey through the sky,
He slows to hide behind the clouds;
This royal orb rules heaven high
And bathes the realm in cleansing shrouds.
The ritual is ever stark,
Repeat the pattern without pause;
Horizon quests from dawn to dark
Is faithful to the domain laws.
A Master King, this solar sphere
Who sits astride his sovereign throne;
Creating shadows far and near
On verdant fields where He has shone.
Oh, Monarchy which magnets Earth
And draws galactic globes and stars,
Give life to every day with birth,
Beget auroral avatars.

Fish Story

There once was a trout in the brook
Who swore he would not bite the hook;
But the lure of the bait
Is what sealed his fate —
Much to the delight of the cook!

Cocoon

Sit I ever caught up in the web of
my own prison,
Woven from the failures and shortcomings
of the past.
Will time release this captive soul to
rise above despair,

Or shall I always be enchained behind this
veil of sorrow
To fade away and die — alone, within my
tomb of torment?
Elapse the seasons of my sleep and sweep away
the shadows,
Oh, metamorphosis, will beauty e'er emerge from
this dark and ugly shell?

Anatomy of Night and Day

Twilight draws the shades of Dusk
And pins them with a star;
The neon suns of Evening wink
While moonbeams shower tinsel.
The countryside becomes alive
With creatures of the dark,
Stealthfully stirring in the ebony hours.
The reverberant sounds of Nature echo
And bounce against the black velvet,
Telling the world that Night is Knight!
For the period of a heartbeat in Eternity,
Time stands still — then,
Sounds the reveille!
Awake the solar disk!
Phoebus proudly probes the East, and
In finality, the bride awaits
The climax of the Daybreak —
And Dawn is the Damsel!

The Torch

One hundred years ago a torch was lit,
Intent to lead the way to Freedom's door.
A beacon lifted high to benefit
The transient world arriving at the shore.
A symbol which invites the hungered souls
To drink and taste of Life's beatitude;
A place where they can realize their goals,
And fear not that believing would delude.

One must devote some time and thought to peace
To overcome the evils in the land,
And breed compassion so that hate will cease;
Help multi-nations better understand.
So yield when necessary or in doubt,
And pray to God the torch does not go out.

Faith, Hope and Charity

Come times when hearts grow weak
    And dreams become a wraith;
Yet strength will overcome,
    Hold out your hands in Faith.
Some days the skies are bleak,
    With endless fear you cope;
Put trust in Him who cares
    For all you need is Hope.
When you are in despair
    And look for loyalty;
The needs of life are filled,
    God grants you Charity.
So, if you feel forlorn,
    Search with sincerity;
A host of friends you find
    In Faith, Hope and Charity!

The Last Leaf

Suspended in seclusion
At the top of the tree,
Forsaken by all its counterparts,
One lone leaf trembles in the breeze.
Preoccupied and apprehensive of
The pending journey,
Clings it perilously to the
Lofty perch, waiting.
Lonely at the top, and in the
Starkness of the solitude,
Life drains from its veins;
The last leaf releases its grasp,
Then flutters downward slowly.
The branches, bare of their raiments,
Lift their limbs skyward in tribute,
And stand there in vast, silent prayer.

Wishing Well

So many pause as they pass by
And give a pensive look —
To drop a coin and make a wish,
Like in a story book.
It's quite the main attraction to
The generations horde
Who gaze into the mirrored pool
And hope for just reward.
Your penny spent may well be worth
The cost it takes to stop,
For all the treasures you may gain,
Yet never have to shop.
Be it health or worldly riches,
Whatever you desire,
Concentrate and dream away —
Perhaps new heights acquire.
Then as you turn to journey on,
A secret you can tell;
From out the depths a whisper comes,
"To you, I'm wishing well!"

The Rounder

A man tumbled head over heels
For a blonde full of giggles and squeals;
He was no acrobat
When his car got a flat —
So she left him for someone with wheels!

Lilacs

As dusk descends upon the land
A fragrance permeates the air,
And gently lingers until morn
When sated dewdrops nectar share.
All shades of lavender supreme
Unfold among the blues and whites;
The clustered blossoms so profuse
Regale their reign like regent knights.
A masterpiece of artistry
To form a garden or a hedge;
With bouquets, freshen every room

Or daily place on window ledge.
They flourish pompously through May,
These tacit treasures of their time;
But when the season starts to fade
The lacy blooms have passed their prime.
A faint aroma now remains,
Reminder of the days gone by;
And seed pods now which take on shape
Prepare themselves to multiply.

False Love

The proud Texan bragged as he drawl'd
To his mail-order bride, so enthrall'd;
Her tresses were grand
To the touch of his hand —
That's when he found out she was bald!

The Tempo of the Rain

On a bleak and wind-swept night,
The rain comes down in torrents
Driving from its path
The inhabitants of earth.
The foliage of the landscape
Withdraws in shivering torment,
Repulsive is the rain
When its fury is in birth.
The rain comes pitter-patter
On a warm and spring-like day,
A cheerful melody sings a
Welcome to the flowers.
It darts about the garden
In a playful sort of way,
Capricious is the rain when
Displaying mystic powers.
On a quiet summer morn
The rain is gently misting,
Giving forth its moisture to
A thirsty world below.
Each pinnacle of grass quickly
Sates itself by sipping
Refreshment from the flora which
The falling rains bestow.

Miracles

Have you ever gazed at birds in flight
With freedom soar at ease,
Or watched a trailing spider at
The end of its trapeze?
Perhaps the rustle of the grass
As zephyrs lightly play;
The graceful swaying beauty of
Artistical ballet?
The twinkle of a thousand stars
That shine forth in the night;
A cricket with its piercing chirp
Or firefly's blinking light?
The scent of new-mown hay upon
An Autumn early morn;
The peaceful cooing of a dove
Or coyote's howl forlorn?
A nesting bird, the Spring's first hatch,
A tumbling waterfall;
The rainbow in a misty sky
Or redwoods old and tall?
An invocation drifting down,
A gift from Him on high;
The greatest blessing yet by far,
A newborn baby's cry!

Formal Wear

Winter's white sports coat
Creates tall top hats with snow
On rural fence posts.

The Sojourn

I took a trip the other day
Beyond the realm we know.
The tunnel that I drifted through
Was dark beyond compare.
My fears were calmed by a gentle voice

Like a shepherd soothes his flock,
For I was in the company
Of the Master of Paradise.
He showed me all the treasures
And the beauty held in store;
Where eternal is the happiness
When the journey is complete.
"Let not your heart be troubled,"
He said, "For I will come again."
So return I to the earthly temple
To await the rapture call.

The Sentinels

In rapt attention stand they tall and proud,
With arms grotesquely reaching toward the skies.
Their tempered, noble visage testifies
Of multitudes with dignity endow'd.
Yet, silent stature rank commands the crowd
O'er desert plains and foothill region highs.
A host of stately warriors in disguise
Like scarecrows groping blindly for a cloud.

Saguaro, gentle giant of the wild,
August esteem shall reign within your realm.
Let no man speak that you should be defiled,
Remain ye, steadfast legions of the helm.
The admiration awe in mundane child
Reflects your puissance to overwhelm.

The Camera

Through a filmy lens,
I find I'm out of focus;
Life is negative.

Fool's Gold

Be not deceived by the things that you see,
Confuse not the prize which you find;
Many a seeker is fooled by the sight
And driven near out of his mind.
Searching in vain for bonanzas of wealth,
A treasure to have and to claim;
Dazzled by glitter, but cheated by fate,
Has only himself he can blame.
Richness of lode can be false in its yield,
A story well known, often told;
Man does not live just by pleasure and lust,
For all that is gained is fool's gold!

Autumn

Summer has faded but fragrances linger
Seemingly pleading for just one more chance;
Stretching forth fingers to clutch at the beauty
Striving to gain a last fleeting glance.
Colours of Fall parade in pied glory,
Flaunting the richness of each brilliant hue;
Leaves that have fallen lay raked and are burning
Spicing the air with perfumed residue.
Harvested fields lay stripped of their raiment,
Gone is the golden mantle of grain;
And in its stead a vastness of grandeur
With ribbons of furrows marking each lane.
On with the season the mood ebbs in tempo,
The passing fancies of days long gone by;
Though Summer grows dim, just off in the distance
The sweet breath of Autumn's rejuvenate sigh.

High Tide

Oceans lap the shore
And taste the pebbled beach with
Robust appetite.

Sodality

A friend is one who stands by you
When others turn their backs;
That special person at your side
Whose spirit never lacks.
The helping hand is there to guide
And lend support to you;
To cheer the hours and comfort bring
When you are feeling blue.
The fellowship of kindred souls
Should never let you down;
And handclasps of a faithful friend
Will help to ease your frown.
There's nothing that can take the place
Of good old-fashioned trust
When offered in a time of need
And judgments are unjust.
Alignment to you some profess,
Yet, when it comes to acts,
The teflon of their tainted words
Will flake when faced with facts.
They know you not, become aloof,
And at the bitter end,
You realize the value of
A true and caring friend.

Flight Path

The black and yellow
Bumble bee, buzzing in flight,
Leaves behind a drone.

God's Graffiti

The ebony matte of the universe
Forms the backdrop for time and place,
When the brush of the Master Painter
Spawns diamonds into space.
The velvet void bursts forth to glow

As the sequined Milky Way,
Transcending through the darkness
Where comets come to play.
His palette fixes sun and moon,
The Godly Rembrant showers
Confetti on one special sphere
And covers it with flowers.
He paints a cloud above it all,
Then rains the oceans full;
Creates the fishes in the seas,
The soaring lark and gull.
He lounges back to view his prize
Then hurls some hues below,
And in an arc they settle to
Beget the first rainbow.
The final stroke — Humanity
Is formed in His own image,
And as they lift their arms in praise
The blessings merge in marriage!

Study in Life Lines

As crispness of Fall hangs in the air,
The hues of Autumn adorn the countryside.
With a blush of colour pulsating through their veins,
A host of leaves cascades down to
Carpet the roots of the parent trees.
Stripped of their raiment, grotesque and skeletal,
Stand they stark, bared limbs groping skyward.
Winter draweth nigh as the nightwinds howl;
Thus, slumber captures the huddled mass of stick trees.
In the throes of the season, dawn awakes;
Statuesque sentinels clad as virgin brides,
Await the espousal kiss of Spring.
Pregnant with anticipation, metamorphosis travails
And with a burst of labored energy comes rebirth!
New leaf kernels emerge in budding transformation;
Regeneration offers its innocent infancy to the world.

Alarm Clock

A cocky rooster,
Feathers ruffled, stretches and
Crows with pride at Dawn.

Riparian Beauty

In the depths of the virgin forest
Where the sunlight is filtered beam,
The breast of the gentle landscape
Is cleavaged to form a stream.
Plundered not by the hand of man
Or bemused by a maiden's blush,
Meandering crystal rivulet
In the midst of the verdant lush.
Flowerlets adorn the placid banks
As the ferns spread their lacy floss;
And the vines of the peaceful woods
Take root in the spongy moss.
The tranquil site is truncate and meek
As it snuggles down to nap
On the carpeted sylvan bedstead
Which is cloaked in a misty wrap.
Dusk overtakes the serenity
And tree prisms fold their limbs;
With their crowns bowed in adoration,
Night breezes hum nocturnal hymns.

Butterflies

Graceful wings of multicolor
Flitter through the air,
Frosted with a coat in velvet
Rainbow shades of flair.
Testing every flower for nectar
Sating appetite,
Flutter off to seek new pleasures
In the warm sunlight.
Polka dots and tiger stripes of

Psychedelic hues,
From the brightest reds and yellows,
Pastel greens and blues.
So breathtaking shapes and sizes,
Varied in design —
Graces Eden's paradise, a
Garden so divine.
Fragile insect, life span wanes as
Tides of time run short;
Grains of sand through Nature's hourglass
Beauty will abort.
But cocoon birth reproduction
Propagates its kind,
Metamorphosis permits new
Worlds to seek and find.

The Lady and The Rogue

Without any warning he entered her life,
A chance introduction, at most;
A man well acquainted with ways of the world,
Egotistic, immodest with boast.
Her infatuous smile and twinkling brown eyes,
He found himself drawn to her side,
Captivated by charm and innocent ways,
Time with her he'd gladly abide.
He approached her with some of his small talk
And asked if she'd share the next dance;
Accepting his bid, she was swept to his arms,
Their closeness admonished by glance.
Then he came on quite strong as the waltz played,
Most surely, this damsel would yield
To the talents he held in abeyance
'Til this point so aptly concealed.
But lure as he tried, she would not succumb,
Instead his advances fell short,
He was caught so off guard, his conquest was lost,
Their relation lacked depth and rapport.
A quizzical look came into his eyes
And he studied her face for a while
For the words she had spoken befuddled his thoughts,

And he grinned an awkward-like smile.
"You see," said she, "I'm free to no man,"
His countenance changed to a frown;
"Nor am I a person that money can buy,"
Then, glanced he suspiciously down.
Quickly regaining composure of mind,
He countered with, "What is your price?"
To which she replied, "True love is a gift
Not decided like rolls of the dice.
The giving and taking of love is a joy,
A privilege reserved for the just;
A treasure to hold and a blessing to have,
Confuse not the symptoms with lust.
Love must have meaning and feelings sincere,
To your ownself, forever be true;
For love is a merger of dreams and of lives,
A reciprocal sharing by two!"

Alpine Frock

River cleavages
Project their bosomed mountain
Peaks, clad in snowcaps.

Magic Wand of Nature

Nature waves her magic wand
And Autumn flaunts its wares;
Wild beasts don their winter coats
Or hibernate in lairs.
Creatures of the wild seek rest,
Some burrow deep beneath;
Others hide within themselves
And weave an armor sheath.
Calmness falls upon the scene
As blankets spread their down;
Trees defrocked of raiment leaves
Adorn a frigid gown.
Seasons tide and in the warmth,
A world in slumber stirs;

Birds and bees and butterflies
Resound in overtures.
Tulips with their bouncing heads
In waltz-time sway in dance,
Fashioned to the Summer march
By colours that enhance.
Dress parades in strutting steps
Cavort as a ballet;
Nature's magic wand conducts
A repeat roundelay!

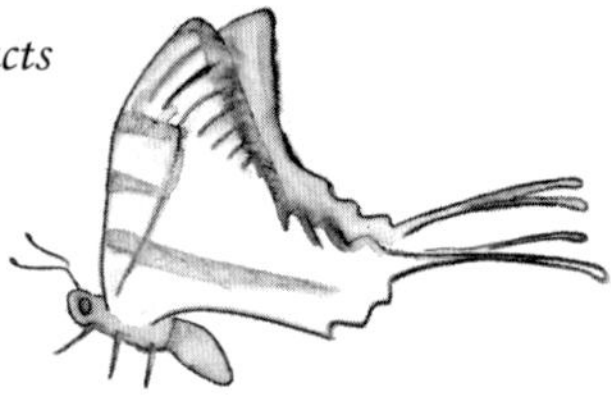

The Search

Where is the peace so sought by man
For countless generations?
Where is the quiet solitude
Desired by multi-nations?
Tranquility escapes the lot
In endless lusting greed,
Serenity cannot be found
To sate the age-old need.
So blinded by their prejudice,
They forge on in their quest;
Where are the placid havens where
The broken souls can rest?
Go seek the land called Paradise,
Contentment so sublime,
Where balm will ease the worldly pains
And slow the hands of time.
Look further all ye brethren,
Depart that lofty perch;
Just bow your heads in penitence,
The goal will end your search!

Airships

Set afloat on high,
The cloud puffs traverse the sky
Adrift like boat fleets.

A Hero for Our Time

For six long days a Nation prayed with hope
And search crews battled time in solemn guise.
Their faithful toils kept spirits on the rise
While rifled foe sought hard to interlope.
As cattle grazed upon the grassy slope,
In solitude an Airman scanned the skies.
To break the silence now would not be wise;
He must await his chance, be patient, cope.

The clock ticks on, salvation must come soon.
Then airwaves crackle, brave men, valor-shod
Take to the air in moments opportune —
At dawn, the rescue snatch from fog-scured sod.
A World proclaims a gallant one is hewn;
No hero, he, he justly credits God!

Scott O'Grady (Spokane, WA)
Desert Storm

The Winds of March

When snows of winter melt away
And thoughts drift by of Spring,
A rise and fall of season tides
The waves or March winds bring.
Unsettled weather everywhere,
Days set in stormy hue;
Clouds hurry-scurry overhead,
Their journey never through.
In open fields some youngsters play
With kites aloft on high,
Preoccupied with trips abroad
'Til twilight time is nigh.
Like fishermen who draw their nets
They reel their prizes in,
And talk about the frolic days
The winds of March begin.
The dormant lawns awake to don

A verdant carpet floor,
Preparing for the great event
Which Nature has in store.
While gusty gales abate and die,
New growth on elm and larch
Look forward to the advent time
Brought by the winds of March.

Portraits

The rainbows of Life
Are reflections painted through
The prisms of years.

U.S. Safari

As I travel through this Nation,
So many sights I see;
While on the trail in Washington,
A Cougar pounced on me!
In the land of corn and honey
On the fields of Iowa;
I milked a Holstein in the field
To quench my thirst away!
Midst the back woods of New England,
In the self-defense and pain;
I had to shoot a Caribou,
Then flee the state of Maine!
Through the hills out in Montana,
I snaked my way in brush;
An Anaconda coiled itself
And squeezed me with its crush!
From a Buffalo I skinned hides
In up-state old New York;
Fixed a steak with all the trimmings,
So pass the knife and fork!
On a trip up to the north woods,
A fishing I did go;
Caught a Salmon in the river
Way up in Idaho!

Flying high above the Rockies,
An Eagle soared for peace;
Settled down in Colorado
Where cares for him will cease!
For a Fossil bed I hunted,
But found an Antelope;
Out in Oregon's wild country
Just off the Cascade slope!
Once a Hereford called upon me
In Texas, tempting fate;
It was late and I was hungry,
So he graced my dinner plate!
These adventures all behind me
I'll rest my head on Plains;
Like the beasts found down in Georgia,
Each Stately creature reigns!

Lost Riches

Silence is golden, or so they say,
But that is all just a joke.
Wealth should be mine by my tacity,
Instead, I am always broke!

The House

There it stands enshrouded in
its cloak of mystery;
The tangled mass of shrubs
held in captive misery.
Hidden in the gabled framework,
secrets from the past,
And hints of all the fabled tales
may surface now at last.
Darkness settles on the house
and drapes are tightly drawn;
Spirits of some yesteryear
may stalk the halls 'til dawn.
Foreboding shadows, lurking forms,
marked with creaking floors.
Eerie depths of things unknown

accent the slamming doors.
A sudden chill awareness
inhibits mind and soul,
When time stands still and hourly,
you no longer hear the toll.
Can it be the house is haunted
by some hostile evil curse
Which envelops those who enter,
and possesses them, or worse?
But perhaps the dwelling seeks a
simple answer of its own,
Like freedom from intrusion
or to just be left alone.
A structure held in torment,
for rumors you can't douse,
One may never solve the riddle,
the enigma of the house!

Gladiola

Begotten from a tiny bulblet
Warmth of Spring promotes a corm,
First a sprig, then stately spikelet
Watch it grow and take on form.
As the rows project their stature
In anticipated hope,
Ever changing shape and pattern
Such as a kaleidoscope.
Reigning in a field of colour
Holding high its princely head,
Gently sways with playful zephyrs
Waltzing in a flowery bed.
Lofty stalks stretch toward the heavens
Reaching for the Summer sky,
Florets bursting forth in beauty
Bring enhancement to the eye.
In its season, Autumn debuts,
Colours of the garden fade;
Nature runs a proper course,
Ends its yearly masquerade.
Miracle of reproduction
Taking place beneath the earth,
In majestic infancy
Labors for a Spring Rebirth!

Well-Groomed

Her parents would not give consent,
Their doubts in her choice every linger;
So, sneak down the ladder she went,
Returning with rings on her finger!

Rebirth

My heart weeps and within shall surely die
the soul of my being.
Gone, faded away is the dream so long held,
cherished, and now lost;
Lost forever in the locked chambers of a dead
and lifeless heart.
I have searched endlessly for an Eden, the
place wherein lies the key;
The key which unlocks the richest treasure of all,
the treasure of love.
Grasping and holding to a fragment thereof,
I see it slip away.
Likened to a wisp of smoke from a flame which
once glowed brightly,
It now smolders in the ashes of things
charred and spent.
Look I for something to soothe a pain which
is worse than death.
From whence cometh the healing balm to
ease my aching heart?
Lift I now my eyes to heaven and gaze upon Him,
the Creator of Love itself.
Therefrom stretches a cool and healing hand,
and I find myself comforted.
Once again life takes on meaning, and with His
love, I shall survive.

Spectacles

Life can remain drab
Even though you hide behind
Rose-colored glasses.

Challenges

Have you ever looked back as you travel
Down the highways and byways of Life
Just to ponder and muse at the turmoil
That is founded in conflict and strife?
When you meditate deep in your psyche
Give some pause to reflect for awhile;
But to face all those challenges daily,
Seek that plateau on high with a smile.
As the riddle unravels about you,
Though the path may be dreary or dark,
Many crossroads are left to your choosing —
Set your sights and take aim at the mark.
Cast your eyes to the heavens above you,
Is the sun on the rise or the set?
What's ahead or behind is your fortune
And depends on the answer you get.
Search for comfort and hope on the mountain
As you reach for life's coveted goal,
Then the calmness that settles upon you
Is the peace which resides in the soul.

Rainbow

Arcing up then arcing down,
Prism colours to behold;
Treasures offered for a crown,
Which way to the pot of gold?

Season of Discontent

Open the portals of presence —
A snowy world dawns like a fresh new day.
The frozen fog clings to the lofty limbs
and points its futile fingers.
Distorted objects watch to witness
the espousal unification;
And the virgin snow bride awaits her
altar sacrifice.

Tethered fence posts stand in rapt
attention wearing marshmallow hats,
While wisps of smoke curl up and
trail across the wintry plain.
Enshrouded shrubs masquerade in disguise
beneath the dune drifts like aliens.
Hark! The breath of Spring caresses
the majestic land!
Ice castles shimmer and the crystal
cathedrals melt into dissipation.
King Winter exhales and is dead —
Long live the Queen!

The Clock

To be wound up with time on your hands,
While seconds are ticking away;
The alarm sounds, so smile with your face
Marking twenty-four hours each day!

Serendipity

While strolling through a hidden rustic glen
I came upon an unexpected scene;
A fawn cavorting with a butterfly
Beneath the filtered rays of sylvan green.
I calmly watched awhile in fascination,
So captivated by what I perceive,
When suddenly my presence is detected,
The magic of the moment takes its leave!
It was, as I recall, up in the attic
When helping Grandma tidy memories;
I found an album full of faded photos,
The pages pictured family histories.
A young girl in a wedding dress reflected
The happiness from many yesteryears;
And as I gazed in awe and adoration,
A mirrored image of myself appears!
While on a visit to a distant city,
An alien, I felt so out of place.

I yearned to be back home with friends and kinfolk
To free myself from all the hectic pace.
I turned to wipe away a lonely teardrop
And seek some solace from the urban maze,
When tender hands reached out to offer comfort;
It was my best schoolmate from childhood days!
So, looking back, the scales of life are balanced,
The pros are equal to the cons, it seems;
Just give a little here — take a little there,
The ups and downs will manifest your dreams.
Go forth, be proud of what you have to offer
Though it may border on simplicity;
To others it could be a God-sent blessing
To share the wealth of serendipity!

Observations from the Deck

The floor of the forest is cushioned with
needles, while the
Staccato rhythms of life beneath
enscroll the carpet;
Native sounds drift among the boughs
like wisps of smoke,
And the fragrances of the season
permeate the air.
Squirrels frolic in a quest to stock
their winter larders
As a bluejay scolds saucily from a
lofty distant perch;
Wild flowers blossom like dotted swiss
on velvet moss.
For a breathless moment a majestic hart
stands motionless at
The edge of the clearing, then bounds off
into his wooded haven.
Sol nods behind the western horizon, and
in the cool dusk
The lanterns of evening are torched in the
darkened heavens.
Peace settles as the shades of night entice
the world to slumber;
A pensiveness encloaks the land and Mankind
sleeps until the morrow.

Diets

Some people are fat while others are thin,
But try as they will to trade places;
The calorie count, a game you can't win,
Like playing without any aces!

Forbidden Love

Love is sin if it should come
To those already pledged;
Even though a breach exists
And lives united, wedged.
Spoken love may long be gone
But yet, its vows do bind;
Hearts may yearn to take the new
And leave the old behind.
Hopes cannot be voiced aloud,
You're bound to solitude;
Comfort comes not to your aid
So dreams bring fortitude.
Pain you suffer — silent grief
From tacit shackling chains;
Kindled sparks have long since died
But still the ash remains.
Life becomes an empty shell,
You dare not reach for stars;
Like a wound of years gone by,
'Tis healed, but leaves its scars.

Random Journey

The paths of time channel their way
Through the tributaries of life,
Leaving a chapter here and there
Reflecting the pleasures or strife.
Like a giant jigsaw puzzle
The mile posts blaze a roadmap trail
With sojourns here and rest stops there,
Itineraries bound to fail.

Branching out to scout the wayside
Seek to chart a new direction,
As sweeping hands upon a clock
Encircle to gain perfection.
One must have a definite goal —
Be sure of the course that you choose,
In lieu, that which you quest for most
May well be the prize that you lose.
Take time — relax — smell the roses,
Let your dreams inspire — don't refute,
Those visions will form new horizons
When the treasured hope seeds take root.
The fruits of your labor abound
In copious harvest of smiles,
For it's not the mileage you make—
Instead, what you make of the miles!

Twilight Years

Being over the hill
Is hard to hide
When your feet are in bedrock
On the far side!

Jacqueline

With spirit and elan you set your goal,
Intent to conquer worlds and turn the tide;
Embark in battle, warrior and his bride,
Life flashing past discreetly bares the soul.
Through shadows in the Vale of Death you stroll,
You're hand in hand with him who's by your side,
Enhaloed at his head to ever guide —
Eternal is the flame, this aureole.

The moon-glade ripples o'er the lake with force
And loosens bonds that ever held their knot.
Your Knight may take the helm and steer the course
Upon the sea of privacy you sought,
For life on earth takes leave without remorse
As restful peace you find in Camelot.

Silent Love

Perhaps I've never said it in
spoken words, as such.
But, then again, some things
cannot be expressed that way.
Maybe a simple mannerism or
a gentle touch or look
Portrays a feeling from deep within
to generate a warm emotion —
A mutual knowledge that the
kindred soul is bound with
An understanding which
mirrors one's feelings.
May the devotion and deep
affection held long in restraint
Break free and surface with
a hope that allows
The heart to release and endear
the love reserved in captive silence.
In other words, I love you.

Split Hairs

Snowcapped mountains crest,
Wearing a fringe of timber
Like a balding man.

International Menu

I have traveled this world over and a
connoisseur am I
Of all the great and tasty food cuisines.
In Europe I have relished sprouts that come
from Old World Brussels,
Then, in Peru, filled up on Lima beans.
What better way to start the day than a plate
of hot French toast
And Danish ham sliced thickly on the side,
Some good old Irish taters laced with
onions from Bermuda,

Topped off by rich Dutch strudel, baker's pride!
I lunched on Polish sausage links stacked high
on Spanish rice, and
Russian salad, Thousand Island dressing;
Hungarian goulash, piping hot, with buttered
English muffins, washed
Down with Bordeaux wine, so effervescing!
In Cologne enfragranced evening, bathed in
Roman candlelight,
A feast of Chinese pheasant under glass,
Italian olives, spiced Swiss chard with Alaskan
king crab salad
And German chocolate cake you can't surpass!
But when the trip is over and you find
yourself back home,
Relax and let your spouse perform the feat;
And as your friends and relatives around the
table gather,
Inform them one and all, "It's now Dutch treat!"

The Gift

The season is upon us
As you scurry on your way,
Looking for that perfect gift
To give on Christmas Day.
You search the counters over
To see if you can find
That special little something
For those you have in mind.
It's a world of tinseled ribbon,
Of flashing lights and wrap
Of green and gold and silver,
Or red garb of "That Chap."
There's the tree and decorations
With an angel at the top;
You can listen to a medley
Of carols while you shop.
While in the distance you can hear
The ringing of the bells,
And the choir at the corner church

Is practicing noels.
Cheerful faces, happy laughter,
All engrossed in joyful dreams,
You're surrounded by enchantment
Of illusion, so it seems.
The commercial art of selling
Has mesmerized mankind
With the hustle-bustle madness
To which everyone's resigned.
Then suddenly you realize
How false the total scene,
And you stop and ask the question,
"What does Christmas really mean?"
'Tis the birthday of the Christ Child
Sent from heaven up above
Given Man in great compassion,
A gesture of eternal love.
For on that Eve so long ago,
As lowly shepherds plod,
Came the greatest present ever,
Hail, the precious Gift of God!

Birthright

Babes conceived in lust
Labor in vain for birth but
Life will never be.

Shadows

Have you ever tried to catch
A shadow while at play
To have it disappear from sight,
Completely fade away?
It reappears across the room
Cavorting on the wall,
While rays of sunlight shower down
To spray a waterfall.
Out in the yard or near a fence,
They linger everywhere —

Elusive as a butterfly
That flits from here to there.
Then dark descends upon the scene
But still they do not wane,
For moonbeams filter through the trees
And dance on windowpane.
Contorted figures plague your dreams
As sleep controls the mind,
Yet, shadows fall across your brow —
There is no peace, you find.

Golden Obsession — The Death of a Star

When the Sunset Years approach
And the breath of Life grows short,
The daily orbit of the Universe is
Likened to the eye of a hurricane —
The lull of the storm — the eddy of
A whirlpool swallowed up by its own nucleus.
An egoist positions itself as the acme peak of
Humanity and looks down upon its subjects below.
With that flair comes isolation
From the nearness of loved ones.
In all Galaxies of the solar system,
When a star burns out, it leaves a black hole,
Devoid of Life, to remain naked and stark
In the lonely solitude of ebony.
The Golden gleam flares and flickers, grows dim,
Then passes into the eternal darkness
From which there is no return.
The craters of the Moon are begotten
By the fallen Stars of yesteryear.

Self-Portrait

My voice may be weak
But my pen strokes portraits in
Hues of a poet.

The Goal

Perhaps as a youngster if you can recall
All the wants and desires in your mind;
Dreams that you had when adulthood you reached
And of all the treasures you'd find.
There would be oceans to sail, mountains to climb
Or the dry desert sands to explore,
Unending adventures of story book lands
With thrills and excitement galore.
Oft straying aside from the origin site
You are dauntless that you shall succeed,
Be it doctor or lawyer or man of the cloth —
Or perhaps do some simplified deed.
You greet each new day as a step to surmount,
See the loftiest peaks to acclaim,
But it's not necessarily heights that you quest
That bring silver or diamonds or fame.
For, happiness comes from the spirit of peace,
Let that guideline inspire and impart;
No goal is too high if you seek it with care
Borne of purity held in the heart.

Indian Summer

'Tis late and the season is tardy,
A haziness hangs in the air;
The harvest lies ready and waiting
For tables to grace with its fare.
Beseechingly, leaves cling to branches,
Embarrassed to multiple shades;
Expecting the Autumnal beckon
When each of them falls in parades.
The lazy reflections are mirrored
And echoed by beasts of the field,
While migrating flocks in the heavens
Pause flights to partake of the yield.
The penchant for pleasures is waning
And summer glides past as a swan;
Like thieves in the night, it is stealing,
Then silently fades and is gone.

In Memoriam

Death leaves only a
Cluster of sweet memories
Sprayed with many tears.

Itinerary

Go get your ticket early for your trip around the world,
Pack your bags and bid the gang, "Farewell."
For you have miles to travel by bus and ship and plane,
Many things to marvel at and tell!
See Cairo, Illinois, drop by Dover, Delaware,
Paris, Texas — Lima, Ohio.
Kentucky offers Warsaw, view Odessa, Washington,
And Rome, New York, or Moscow, Idaho.
Next, head for Athens, Georgia, then to Belfast, Tennessee,
Stockholm, Maine, and Bethlehem, PA.
In Iowa, meet your Waterloo — lunch China, Indiana,
Grace Geneva, Kansas — lounge Lisbon in LA.
Pearl dive Manila, Utah, smoke Havana, Arkansas,
Weigh anchor at Dutch Harbor in Alaska;
Visit Venice, California, cross Jordan to Montana,
Browse Berlin, Mass., or cruise to Crete, Nebraska.
As you travel through the country, see the tribes of Trinidad
In mountains high, way out in Colorado;
Be a matador and stalk the bull and win in old Madrid
Alone while passing through New Mexico.
Shop Sussex in Wyoming, then go to Genoa, Nevada,
There's Lebanon, New Hampshire, and Dublin, Michigan;
Greet Glasgow, West Virginia, bask Bermuda, Alabama,
Smell Cologne up in New Jersey, foggy London, Oregon.
Jaunt to Jamaica, Vermont, or Damascus, Maryland,
Dine in Denmark, South Carolina, fly to Florence, Arizona;
Hail Halifax, Virginia, highland fling in Scotland, Conn.
Bike through Belgium in Wisconsin, party Prague in Oklahoma.
In Jerusalem, Rhode Island, fall to your knees and pray,
Take a nap in Naples, Florida, munch in Munich, North Dakota;
Bridge to Belgrade, N.C., laugh in Luxemburg, Missouri,
Drink scotch in Aberdeen, S.D., frolic Finland, Minnesota.
As you marvel at the worldly sights of deserts far away,

Peer pyramids in Egypt down south in Mississippi;
And when your journey ends, one place will stand apart
While you hula in Hawaii — it needs no foreign city.
Now that your trip is over, you're exhausted by the miles,
But share with friends the joys, their when and where;
Then maybe next time you can make your lengthy tour in peace,
At home relaxed and in your easy chair!

Lilacs

In clustered masses,
Profusion blooms, their fragrance
Wafts upon the air.

Snowflake

Snowflake gently flutters down,
Exclusive pattern each design;
A miracle unmatched by man
Compounding self on shrub and vine.
So delicate this passive lace
And perfect in its artistry,
Yet, fragile to the human touch
Forever longs it to be free.
Catch a snowflake in your hand,
While watching, it will disappear;
Starlet fades into a droplet
Likened to a baby's tear.
As Nature paints a frosty scene
Detailed like those in picture books,
A portrait mass of feather drifts
Which has no duplicate in looks.
In clustered multi mounds of white
Assemble they on countryside,
For mass protection huddled close,
But from their fate they cannot hide.
When sunny Sol breaks forth to glow,
It warms and melts their cold, cold hearts;
Evaporate or hibernate —
Not yet, here come their counterparts!

Cattails

Tomcat walks the fence
Seeking a feline suitor
For a purrfect tale.

The Patriots

The gallant heroes walk through History
Exemplifying freedom for the cause
Of men in search of pacifistic laws
So generations live in amity.
But often in the course is perfidy,
And forces from beyond give vent to pause,
Usurping liberties from out the claws —
Emancipations won so valiantly.

Whence comes the time that powermongers lust,
The bold, the brave, the dauntless congregate.
Espoused courageous guidance of the just,
The evil ones prepare to meet their fate.
Endearment credo says, "In God We Trust,"
For love is ever victor over hate.

The Symbol

I am a remnant of History,
I share your being
And ensure your destiny.
Look back upon the truths I've upheld.
I represent the hopes of Yesterday,
The realities of Today,
And the promise of Tomorrow.
I am your past, your present, your future.
Like the ancestral dreams of your forefathers,
I've proclaimed your pride upon the breeze;
Hung limp, half-mast, as you mourned,
And endured when others succumbed.
I sanction for much, yet demand little;
Just give me your respect and allegiance.
I shall neither desert nor betray you,
But, please, I beseech . . . do not desecrate me.

Used Cars

They say, "Take it for a test drive,"
But how are you to know
If you ride it, herd it, whip it
Just to make it go?
There might be some you shoot or kill
To grace the menu fare;
Do battle with or hide from,
While others you may wear.
So listen to my story,
Decide then for yourself
If it's worth the price that's listed
Per the Blue Book on the shelf.
Look up above the tree tops,
A Skylark can be heard;
See an Eagle and a Falcon,
Or watch a Thunderbird.
Don't take off on the warpath when
The Navaho attack;
Smoke peace pipes with the Cherokee
And scalp not Pontiac.
Be a wrangler, roping Mustangs,
Hunt Rabbits on the range;
Chase Rams high in the mountains,
Fish for barracudas, strange.
Explorers lead Safaris out
In search of Jaguar tracks,
While Wildcats stalk the Caravan,
Impalas race in packs.
In the Galaxy of Heaven
Where Comets come to play;
Look for Mercury and Saturn
In stardust Astro spray.
In Quest of costly fashion wraps
Wear Sables, if you please;
But to relax, you may prefer
A Blazer and Capris.
In Spirit worlds of Silhouettes,
Mirages float in air;
The Accent of the Spectrum hues
Make Shadows flit with flair.

You've searched the car lots over
And driven miles and miles,
Been smitten by the salesman's spiel
And condescending smiles.
Now you have had the chance to shop,
Compared each breed and specie;
You've knuckled down and buckled up,
Been optioned by degree.
Then comes the time they shake your hand,
"Let's make a deal," they say.
But read the fine print well before
You sign your life away!

Autumn

Fall colours exhale
Their final breath, the flames dim,
Then shudder in death.

Halloween

"Tis the day when all the goblins
Host their yearly masquerade;
Witches fly aloft on broomsticks,
Jack-o'laterns fashion made.
Youngsters don their eerie costumes
For a door-to-door demand;
"Trick or Treat," you'll hear them banter,
Snatching treasures at command.
Marching forth like little soldiers
Homeward bound as dark descends;
Clutched in hand their precious cargoes,
Mixed emotions this night lends.
Shadows reach as though to grab them,
Screeching bats dart overhead;
Black cats prowl atop the fences,
Oh, to be at home in bed!
Come the morn they brag of conquest
Over forces they have seen;
How they frightened off the specters
Of another Halloween.

The Winds of Carson Valley

From out the blue a whisper starts,
Then ripples through the skies;
It pauses then to take a breath
And dust the native eyes.
The tumbleweeds are restless now
Like cattle in a storm —
By herding here, stampeding there,
They huddle to keep warm
. . . From the winds of Carson Valley.

A hoarseness in the zephyr's throat
Belies its mild approach;
It gathers speed and gallops fast
To trespass and encroach.
All nature seeks a haven safe,
Protection from the wrath —
Escaping threats of sight and sound
And steer clear from the path
. . . Of the winds of Carson Valley.

In dark of night a chilling screech
Comes whistling through the air;
Mutating all that it confronts,
Distorts without a care.
The mighty giant blusters hard
And gasps a fleeting breath —
The storm exhales its final blast,
Then fades away in death.
. . . Oh, the winds of Carson Valley.

Tributaries

Likened to wayward hanks of hair
Exploring the countryside;
Peacefully, tributaries wend
A path which is etched in pride.
Stretching to stroke a distant shore
Or touch upon foreign soil,
Seeking a haven free from fear,

They toe the mark with their toil.
Treasures lie buried deep within
And course through the passage streams,
Flowing to oceans far away
Fulfilling a host of dreams.
Branching like limbs on family trees
To trail as a vine, so rife;
Goals that are reached reward you in
This journey that's known as life.

Skeletons

From out the closet
Secrets emerge baring their
Sexualities.

The Rose and The Thorn

The briers prick the virgin flesh
and penetrate beyond
To pierce the womb of ecstasy
of visionary dreams.
Crack apart the calyx fist and
stretch the sepal fingers
As furled petals hug themselves
within the pregnant bud.
Loose thyself, unfold — burst forth
in radiant colour,
The perfumed blooms are eager and
blush with expectation.
Kiss the nectared lips offered in
their lavish essence
And taste the dew-moist blossom —
enhance the reverie.
Release the sweet aroma, drink in
the wealth of love,
A world of happiness is open to
the multitude.
Rejoice, oh heart, and nurture in
the beauty of the garden
For a perfect rose cannot be gained
without the harshness of the thorn.

Mourning Dove

The nacre feathers ply upon your breast,
And sad but trusting eyes imparting grace
Peer kindly out from your angelic face.
Tranquility your nature, daily quest,
While sit you gently on a downy nest
And share a lifelong mate in love's embrace.
The opalescent pearls you wear as lace
Create the aura you are saintly blest.

Though life is short, on naught can we depend;
The simple joys and blessings fade and cease.
Togetherness you know comes to an end,
And solo flights aloft entreat release.
Your suffering is shared, my grieving friend,
Mourn not, oh faithful harbinger of peace.

Weeping Willow

Oh, weeping willow must you mourn
In silence and with grief?
Just what is it that bothers you,
Can you not find relief?
Now, are you yearning for a mate,
Perhaps a faithful friend;
And as your catkins show lament,
May I some kindness lend?
The whisper of your muted sobs
Is wafted on the breeze;
And branches sigh in sorrow deep,
You're lonesome midst the trees.
While leaves are drooping in despair
The world will hear your plea,
Though you are sad and lonely there
New hope is stirred in me.
Instead of weeping as you stand
It's praise you wish to share;
Those thousand tossled heads of yours
Are bowed in silent prayer.

Discipline

Naughty child deserves
Love pats to rear in form of
Spank-fire liniment!

Just Dessert

The door is shut, the dye is cast —
A point of no return;
The wall of brick stands firm and tall,
Rewards you justly earn.
To face defeat is bitter when
Each day you search for dawn;
And friends may turn their backs to you
Or use you like a pawn.
Rise up above the darkened veil,
Go seek that inner peace;
Then let the world spin evermore,
Its journey never cease.
The cake is sweet down to the crumb,
You taste each morsel through;
But life is not designed to have
Your cake and eat it, too.

Terminus

When time descends upon this mortal mass,
Don't bind me to this world with tubes and wires.
If the breath within the temple has grown frail,
Release my earthly form of yesterday.
Just loose the tethers, let my soul drift free,
Enshackle not this dead and empty shell.
When life is o'er the spirit longs to soar
And peace embalms the captive memories.

The Breeze

I FEEL you gently stir the air and I am made
to be aware,
The same caress upon my brow gives swaying to
the timbered bough,
Exalting trodden spirits much the world awaits
your tender touch.
I HEAR the whisper of your voice and all of Mankind
can rejoice;
The rustle in the leaves on high reveals the fact
you're passing by
To freshen all in life you brush with quiet
lullabies to hush.
I SMELL your fragrance as you pass and watch the ripple
of the grass
Which undulates in waltz-time grand to permeate
a waiting land;
The docile scent drifts through the dales olfacting perfumes
o'er the vales.
I SEE the birds and butterflies flit through your currents
to the skies
And waft on wings to other worlds reflecting peace
your breath unfurls;
While zephyrs lift the trailing spores to propagate some
new encores.
I TASTE the sweetness you impart, 'tis nourishment for
soul and heart
To quench the thirst and appetite; I drink with
savory delight,
Imbiding in your want to please, I'm sated by you,
phantom breeze!

Loneliness

Perhaps in the midst of a bustling crowd
A sad mood envelops your mind;
The deafening silence is screaming out loud
And to others around you are blind.
Neglected by those who have gone on their way,
Set apart from the scene near at hand;
You grope through the shadows and plead as you pray,
"God, endow me the strength to withstand."
Though time rushes by you, the minutes stand still,
And emotions well up in your eyes;
You yearn for tomorrow, or yesterday's thrill,

But to live for today would be wise.
Yet, loneliness may be a refuge for souls,
Or a place for your spirits to mend;
The haven that heals and appraises your goals
May be just what the heart needs, my friend!

Echoes

Soundwaves drift aloft,
Bouncing back and forth, create
Reverberations.

Kingdoms

The world tempts with vacuous treasures,
While, in fact, it's the goals that you seek
Which make up the course to your future,
Be it ever so bold or so meek.
Accept what life offers, be humble,
For the promise is given to all;
Enhance not yourself with a false pride
As you know, it precedeth a fall.
Dote not on material assets,
They are mortal and surely will fade;
But mansions await all the faithful,
As the earthen ones join the crusade.
A peace passeth all understanding
When it showers from heaven above;
Then blessings will settle upon you
In the Kingdom of eternal love!

Cupidity

Careless Romeo
Stubbed a toe and fell in love
His head over heels.

Tumbleweed

Tumbleweed, where do you come from,
When did your journey start?
What made you such a rambler,
Perhaps a broken heart?
The miles you left behind you
Reflect upon your face.
Must you roam about forever,
Can't you settle down some place?
Won't you pause and rest a moment
Before you wander on,
And give some thought to what's ahead,
The past is by and gone?
Are you searching for a treasure,
Or perchance a long-lost friend?
Consider what's around you,
Will your travels never end?
You're as restless as a whirlwind
Astir with every breeze,
Uneasiness your nature
Like a hive of swarming bees.
Weathered by life's struggle, you're
Off again in endless flight;
Not a single word is heeded
As you tumble out of sight.

What Price Glory

To soar with eagles was her heart's desire,
For wings could help fulfill her every dream;
The acme call would give her joy supreme
While saintly garment clouds provide attire.
Untethered, floating free, the skies inspire,
"I'll fly until I die," her motto theme,
To sing the lofty praises of esteem
Which echo of the holy angel choir.

A child entranced in glee by all the mirth,
The heavens as a stage to play her role.
Above the realm of mortals tied to earth,
Her heart is loose to seek that starry goal.
Now, human hands that held her close at birth
Release into the arms of God her soul.

Jessica Dubroff
5/5/88 to 4/11/96

Poetry to Me is . . .

Expressions of the elations and depressions of the soul
. . . zealous goal.
Release of the pent-up emotions of one's psyche,
. . . oh, spirit free.
Sharing of impassioned visions and desires,
. . . each inspires.
Artful music of Picasso or Rembrandt portraited in verse,
. . . chords rehearse.
Effervescent laughter, the glisten of misty eyes,
. . . dreams realize.
Perfect merging of Day and Night into forever,
. . . ending, never.
The stroking and caressing or words on artistry's harp,
. . . astutely sharp.
Vibrations of songbirds or the aroma of a thousand flowers,
. . . breathless hours.
The rejuvenation of birth or the finality of death,
. . . fleeting breath.
The arabesque of Life woven from aurora unto sunset,
. . .voice vignette.
An ability to blend all these into a great symphony,
. . . perfect harmony.
Finding beauty in all things . . . is poetry to me!

Why Me?

Have you ever looked back at life and then asked,
"Why was I singled out for this cross?"
While the trail has been long, and heavy the load,
Yet, you struggle, your mind at a loss.
Tribulations and trials prey on your soul,
But in silence you suffer with grief.
Then as time passes by, the visions will fade
And you call out and beg for relief.
When you give it some thought, it's written and said
That your lot's no more than you can bear;
Inner strength may be gained from burdens in life
And your victories others now share.
You might count it a blessing, chance in disguise,
For you cannot change what is to be —
So, just give of yourself, your talent, your love,
And your question is answered, "Why me?"

Pussywillows

Soft tufts of velvet
Grace the intricate branches,
Purring in the breeze.

The Songbird Singeth

The pinnacled glow of Phoebus
heralds the early hours of morn.
The trees awaken and stretch their limbs
and shake their tresses lightly.
. . . Dawn stirs. And the songbird singeth.

All is bright and the happy sounds
of Nature fill the air.
The flowers with open faces drink
of life in acquiescence.
. . . Rejoice! For the songbird singeth.

The day matures and prudently
advances towards its terminus,
A time when the vespers of Morpheus
beget a lullaby.
. . . Dusk falls. And the songbird singeth.

Fall Trees

There's a time when the trees of the forest
Shed the mantle of green which they wear,
And don the bright colours of Autumn
To carpet the woods' thoroughfare.
Mother Nature has chosen their costume
Selected with infinite grace,
And has given them a new countenance
By painting a smile on their face.
Then slowly, the leaves flutter downward,
Leaving the branches all bare;
The trees lift their arms toward Heaven
And stand there in vast, silent prayer.
Thus, they give praise to their Maker,
And await the arrival of Spring,
When the slumbering heart shall awaken
To burst forth in colour again.

Pansies

Delicate faces
Of psychedelic hues laugh
With distorted grins.

A Ribbon for Anthony

A blessing to his home, this boy of ten,
So loved by all his family and peers;
A child at heart, yet wise beyond his years,
Displaying youthful trust and acumen.
Respectful of each fellow citizen,
He sets his goal, like early pioneers;
With peace of mind, the Master quells his fears,
In praise of God he echoes an, "Amen!"

But life is full of predators who wait
To steal the joy and alter destiny;
Their senseless acts create contempt and hate,
Yet faith consoles and lets the soul drift free.
"Defile not," loved ones plead, "Do not berate,
Wear yellow ribbons in his memory."

In Memoriam of Anthony Michael Martinez

Ode to a Saint

Hark, I hear the sonic boom of
Yonder mount awaking.
A Sunday morn is shattered, and
History's in the making.
Belching forth the pressures from
Its bowels deep within,
Beast and mankind buried, never
To be seen again.
The plume cloud spews the ashes on
A dormant countryside,
Those caught beneath its sediment
Can find no place to hide.

A trail of devastation cuts a
Path throughout the West
As darkness of a thousand nights
Expands out from the crest.
Your restlessness has all but driven
Life-long friends away
Lamenting those who died upon the
Eighteenth day of May.
With magma rising in your throat
And threats to ever drool,
Oh, raging beauty, when will you
Retire and temper cool?

Friendship's Garden

Gazing in the mirror of reflected bygone years
To the cultivated garden of my youth;
The blooms may fade or blossoms die,
But friendships linger on
And echo in the reminiscent mind.
Shrinking violets are likened to the meek and mild,
The timid tacit fellowships of yore;
Lilting laughter wafts upon the titillating breeze
To splash in puddles of forgotten smiles.
Kindred souls of yesterday, like lilies in the field,
Sway gracefully in wistful reverie;
Stop and smell the roses which enhance the joys of time,
And resound rhapsodic scents of amity.
Vines trail through the countless years
And cling to loving hearts,
Aromas permeate and spice the dreams.
Life is ever nectared by sweet memories recalled
And perfumed by the fragrances of friends.

Sequoia

Mighty maestros standing tall
With spires that stroke the sky;
Templed timber boughs outstretched
Caress and kiss the clouds.

Herded high upon the hills
These gentle giants grow;
Misty morns shroud lofty limbs
In passive puissance.

Harken to hushed harmony
Found from the forest floor;
Crested canopies create
An air of awe above.

Tensiled trees in prayerful praise
Endure Eternity!

Fashion Parade

Frocks of frozen fog
Cloak forested mountains and
Create crystal spires.

We Shall Survive

(September 11, 2001)

Our cities rent by friendly wings
  From rubble, rise once more;
The sky-jacked tools you utilized
  Were instruments of war.
While skylines alter in a flash
  Our nation's creed won't change'
You may tear away at structures,
  But faith's not out of range.
Though wounds can separate the land
  The mass you can't divide;
You concentrate on terror,
  But Praise God, He's on our side!
The flags hang limp at half-mast

And tears be-dim the eyes;
In God we trust when clouds depart
Our battered banner flies.
The torch held high out in the bay
Shows courage in its reign;
Holds forth the freedom of the land
Where liberty won't wane.
No weakness in Old Glory's wave
Her twinkling stars behold;
The stripes of crimson red and white
Pride worn with mantle bold.
Let History reflect the plight
Of how the people strive;
With heads held high, their battle cry
Proclaims, "We shall survive!"

Rainbows

Prism colours arc
To span the far horizon,
Yielding pots of gold.

Accept Me as I Am

Accept me as I am —
For to change me would make me someone I am not.
If you do not like me as I am —
Do not make demands or offer me sympathy.
My world is small, but all I desire
Is to be a part of that world.
My demeanor is my strength, my armor;
It shields me from the real world.
You may call it attitude — others call it spunk!
I cannot compete in your world at your level;
That which is a simple accomplishment to you
May be a monumental achievement to me!
Mentor me, but do not master me.
Counsel me, but do not control me.
Befriend me, but do not betray me.
Encourage me, but do not encompass me.
I must be the way I am
To make up for my own failures or shortcomings.
To change, I would cease to exist...
So, accept me as I am.

The Ballade of Pacifica

The nectar blooms of peach and pome
Waft gently o'er the slopes on high;
While forests teem with humus loam,
Their sylvan spires caress the sky:
Where eagles soar with eager eye
And stately fronds of fern abound;
The mushroom spores take wing and fly . . .
Tread softly, you're on sacred ground.

Where northern spotted owls call home
And stealthy cougars claw and pry;
The legendary Sasquatch roam,
Coyotes howl their mournful cry.
As coulees grand gorge wet and dry;
A river cleaves, its waters pound,
But warm Chinooks can petrify . . .
Tread softly, you're on sacred ground.

When Mount Saint Helen split its dome
The patchwork fields of grain lay nigh;
And beaches of the Sound lapped foam
Where undulating breezes sigh.
All things must ultimately die,
And templed orisons resound
When men no longer need to vie . . .
Tread softly, you're on sacred ground.

For peace of mind you cannot buy
Tranquility has oft been found.
Yet, through it all, we wonder, "Why?" . . .
Tread softly, you're on sacred ground.

Lion's Pride

Like beasts found in the jungle
In search of captive prey;
We set our sights on members
To visit us — then stay!
We shake their hands in friendship
And tell them of our goal;
Present them each a challenge
To strengthen heart and soul!
We stalk the enemies of sight
Then help the deaf to hear;
Providing hope to those in need
To let them know we're near!
As dedicated Lions
The youth we guide with care;
So they may know they're precious;
Our wisdom, freely share!
By taking aim at ignorance,
Be visible — don't hide;
For when you are a Lion
Declare, "WE CARE," with pride!

In view of the fact that I am an active member of a local Lions Club, the largeset Service Organization in the world, LCIF (Lions Club International Foundation), the above poem was written as a tribute to the organization.

Lion Betty A. Cleek,
Melvin Jones Fellow

Poetry in Song

The following pages contain a select group of my earliest poetic efforts which were composed in the form of songs.

In that most of them are products of the 1940's, some of them reflect the effects of the war years. Perhaps they are dated and passe' by today's standards, but they had meaning and gave vent to emotions for their day.

I have endeavored to give a broad spectrum, and diversity in these poem songs. They range from inane to tragedy, ballad to love song. Most were written prior to age 20 years, so the ideas are viewed from the eyes of a youth growing up during World War II.

Without the benefit of music (I neither read nor write music), perhaps you can visualize them set to music. Each selection has a distinct melody to enhance the lyrics as they appear here, and I have footnoted them with the date of composition.

Hopefully, you will enjoy this phase of my poetic growth while it was in its infancy.

EmCee Kown

The Rocking Horse

His rocking horse stands in the corner
To frolic in fun nevermore;
Our son is now grown and a soldier
Out fighting to help win this war.
He joined up the day that the Japs took Bataan,
We all hope and we pray he will come back again.
Just imagine our joy when he walks in the door
He will be home forever to leave us no more.

We received a letter this morning,
So happy are we when we hear;
Our dear one was fine but was wishing
That all of his loved ones were near.
He said he was healthy but lonesome for us,
I guess that's only natural, he loves us so much;
He then mentioned his Buddy and said he must close
'Cause the Nippos are coming and "God only knows."

His rocking horse stands in the corner,
"Leave it there 'til I'm back," he said.
The telegram came just this evening
Informing us our son is dead.
He gave up his life so that others may live,
And he gave up his freedom, what more can he give?
I guess that God knows what's best, so if it had to be,
Please watch over our Nation, may it always be free!

(January, 1944)

Daisies Will Tell

If your love seems uncertain
And you don't know what to do,
Just listen as I give you some advice.
Don't go to fortunetellers,
There's a simpler way for you,
So try it without even thinking twice.

Daisies will tell if she loves you,
Daisies will tell if she don't.
Other flowers may be pretty,
But telling fortunes they won't.
"She loves me, she doesn't,
She loves me, she does."
That's what the daisy told me.
Daisies will tell if she loves you,
Go pluck a daisy and see!

(February, 1944)

Teardrop Waltz

How we danced and romanced
In the moonlight
To the beautiful Teardrop Waltz.
How we lived, how we loved
On that June night
To the strains of the Teardrop Waltz.
But I didn't know that
It never could be;
I loved you so, and I
Thought you loved me.
Now I sit here alone
In the moonlight
Hating the Teardrop Waltz.

(November, 1950)

Lilacs in the Rain

Lilacs in the rain,
Memory's refrain
Bring back the days of yore.
When the skies were blue,
They were blue for you,
You've gone and they're gray once more.
My heart is lonely, Dear,
I long to have you near.
Please come back again
And chase away the rain.
Then, with lilacs in the sun,
My life has then begun,
You're back in my arms as before.

(December, 1947)

The Convict's Last Request

The clock just chimed eleven
Upon that fateful night;
The warden sat serenely at his desk.
His face was drawn and haggard
As he gazed into the eyes
Of a convict who had made his last request.
For later in the darkness,

Just at the stroke of twelve,
This man before him was condemned to die.
He pleaded with the warden
To listen to his tale
And keep his secret as the years go by.
I have a wife and daughter
Way down in San Antone;
I left them, oh, so many years ago.
I told them I'd come back again,
But never kept my word,
Just promise that you'll never let them know.
It would break their hearts to learn
The vows I made to them
Were broken by the man that they loved best.
My time on earth is waning
So I'll beg you once again,
Please hear my plea and grant my last request!
(May, 1947)

Let's Start the New Year Right

Another year has passed
With tears and laughter, too.
But here's some good advice
To follow all year through.
Be good and kind and share
Your happiness of heart;
The New Year's coming soon,
And that's the time to start.
Let's start the new year right
With love, good will and peace.
Say thanks with all your might
For war and strife to cease.
Forever, now we pray
That freedom stays in sight,
So, once again I say,
"Let's start the New Year right."

(October, 1945)

Lollapalooza Sue

Lollapalooza Sue,
She comes from Kalamazoo.
She's hep to the jive and man alive,
There's nothing she can't do!
Then, there's Lou from Louisiana,
She's really quite a chick.
But it's Lollapalooza Sue, my boys,
That makes your ticker tick!
She's got beaux in every city
From The Bronx to San Jose'.
They all think her very pretty
With a name that's hard to say.
Now you take Sally from the valley,
With beauty ever so rare.
But my saucy little Suzie,
To her you can't compare!

(July, 1943)

Untrue Kisses

Untrue kisses are what you gave me,
Making love that wasn't fair.
Untrue kisses, who could blame me
For believing that you care?
Once you told me that my kisses
Meant the world and all to you,
But I find now to my sorrow,
That your kisses were untrue.

(October, 1949)

Love is Just a Game

Love is just a game
As far as you're concerned,
With broken hearts the goal of every kiss.
I played along with you,

But too late now I find
That tears are my reward instead of bliss.
I've always been a good sport
In every game I played,
But you cheated and you lied
For all the honest moves I made.
Love is just a game
It's something that you feign;
I lost the match, I'll never love again.

(September, 1949)

The Guitar Waltz

Just listen and you'll hear a haunting melody,
It's sweet and low, you'll like it 'cause it's heavenly.
Reminds me of the happy days that have gone by.
I wish that you were here, I wish that you were near,
And that we'd never said, "Goodbye."
The Guitar Waltz, The Guitar Waltz,
Just lingers on and on.
I'll ne'er forget the night we met,
It happened through that so-o-ong.
I hear it now, the waltz that made the lovelight shine,
But only tears can fill these lonely eyes of mine.
I wish that you would give me just one chance and then,
I know that my poor heart would get a second start,
That waltz would be our song again.

(January, 1948)

The Locket

My Mother died so many years ago,
Her memory still lingers on and on.
She gave to me this tarnished golden locket
Which has her name engraved and etched upon.
It's just a simple little piece of jewelry,
But something with which I will never part;
My Mother's picture is inside this locket,
I'll always carry it next to my heart.

A year or so ago I got in trouble,
I don't know what I did it for.
They linked me to a crime in old Chicago,
And sent me up for twenty years or more.
I have nothing to do but sit around,
Waiting for the day when I am free.
My Mother's locket still is in my pocket,
I pray to God above she did not see!

(October, 1945)

The Stars in Your Eyes

The stars in your eyes shine down on my heart
And tell me that you'll be true.
Your lips whisper low that we'll never part,
As the moon plays tag with the dew.
Then after a while, you stray from my arms,
I'm left all alone here to pine.
Now, the stars in your eyes shine down on the heart
Of the one who was broken mine.

(June, 1949)

I'll Never Love Again

I'll never love again
Because I can't have you.
It isn't fair, I know,
But, Dear, what can I do?
I loved with all my heart,
And now there's only pain.
Because I can't have you,
I'll never love again.

You let me think you cared,
I fell in love with you.
But now you're gone and I'm
Alone and feeling blue.
I built my castles high,
But built them all in vain.
Because I can't have you,
I'll never love again.

(October, 1949)

Cherokee Polka

There's a dance that they're doing down Texas way,
It started in a little town in I-O-WAY.
Stomp your left foot, then your right, do as I say,
. . . Cherokee Polka!
Turn around and chase your partner to and fro,
Watch him dart about, he knows just where to go.
Look into his eyes and see the light aglow,
. . . Cherokee Polka!
Pass right through, balance two,
Swing your partner 'round.
Let him know you won't let go,
Then courtsey to the ground.

That's the dance that they're doing out in Cheyenne,
From there across the country and then back again.
It's the favorite of the ladies and the men,
. . . Cherokee Polka!

(March, 1947)

Love Insurance

I'm going to take out love insurance
To protect myself from you;
I'll get a great big policy
In event you are untrue.
It's sure to pay rich dividends
With double indemnity
In case of accidental death
Of the love you promise me.

There are times when love is risky,
Perils loom on every turn;
But protected with insurance,
I'm assured of a return.

So, I'll pay a monthly premium
Which provides a good supply
Of love and hugs and kisses
To last until I die.

(October, 1953)

When a Little Boy Cried

A little boy's cry
Was heard in the night;
The reason is clear,
His Dad was off to fight.
Through his sobs you can hear
His prayer to Him above;
"Bless my Daddy, oh, God,
Bring him back to our love."
A little boy's laugh
Was heard in the air;
His Daddy was home
From the war over there.
That night while in his bed,
"I'm thankful," he then sighed,
God heard everything
When a little boy cried.

(June, 1944)

There's a Smile on Your Face

There's a smile on your face
But there's tears in your eyes,
Please tell me why you're blue.
Am I making you glad
Or making you sad
By asking that you be true?
It hurts me so to see you cry,
What am I to do?
There's a smile on your face
But there's tears in your eyes,
And those tears break my poor heart in two.

(October, 1949)

The Hopeless Cowboy

I'm just a bowlegged cowboy with pigeon toes,
I wear a hat to cover up my nose.
My shoes don't fit me and my shirt's too long,
I ride around the ranch just singing this song,
"I ain't got a pal, I ain't got a gal,
I ain't got a dime to my name.
But I want a pal and I want a gal
So I can change her name."
My ears are floppy and my eyes don't match.
There's three fingers missing but I'll get a new batch.
My nose is crooked, but I don't care
'Cause whatever I've got, I'm willing to share!

(August 1944)

Washington Waltz

I can hear that haunting waltz of the Northland
    And it brings back the days I knew.
Of all the happy hours that I spent there,
    Happy because there was you.
Now, I yearn for my Washington sweetheart,
    And long to see her again,
But as days come and go,
I've found out to my woe,
    That my love for her's all been in vain.

(January, 1948)

When it Comes to Love, I Strike Out

When it comes to love, I strike out,
    Every dog-gone time.
When I think I've made a hit with you,
    You substitute with mime.
I think, "Tonight's the night for sure,
    Victory I will claim,"
But when I start to pitch some "woo,"

You up and call my game.
Instead of stealing bases,
I'd like to steal your heart.
And make a run for home with it,
Where we would never part.
But, that would be an error,
I'd get the boot, no doubt.
For when it comes to love, my dear,
That's when I strike out!

(July, 1950)

The Face of an Angel

'Twas only a dear babe of four,
This story her life will unfold.
Her eyes were as bright as the stars,
Her hair, the color of gold.
One night as twilight was falling,
Her mother had gone into town,
She left me to care for our darling,
Without even showing a frown.

The creek that runs down to the mill,
Flows gently, but swift past our door.
Our daughter was taught ne'er to stray,
To the edge of its dangerous shore.
That night as she knelt by her bedside,
A blue ribbon tied in her hair,
She looked like an angel from heaven.
Her beauty was ever so rare.

Later that night without thinking,
I went for a stroll down the lane.
If only I'd known all the heartaches,
The sorrow, the tears and the pain.
It seems that our daughter so cherished,
Got up and had walked in her sleep.
For early next morning we found her,
So lifeless and dead in the creek.

The blue eyes that once were so bright,
Forever are closed to this land.
The ribbons that held back her hair,
Are damp to the touch of my hand.
Her face is still that of an angel,
So restful, so peaceful and fair,
Her soul has risen to heaven,
Where she is awaiting us there.

(February, 1946)

EmCee Kown, born Betty Ann McKown, March 1, 1929, at Rialto California, became permanently wheelchair bound from polio at the age of eleven (1940) while a resident of Cherokee, Iowa. She lived most of her adult life in the Pacific Northwest—namely, Medical Lake and Spokane, Washington, with sojourns at Mountlake Terrace, Washington, and Hemet, California. She currently is a permanent resident of Tucson, Arizona.

Publications Credits and Awards:

Anthologies:
World of Poetry
American Poetry Association
Watermark Press
Arcadia Poetry Press
Cader Publishing, Ltd.
Amherst Society
National Library of Poetry
Iliad Press
Potomac River Poetry Consortium
Sparrowgrass Poetry Forum, Inc.
Creative Arts & Science Ent.
Famous Poets Society
Poetry Guild
Quill Books

Recognitions:

Listed 1989 and 1992 "Who's Who in Poetry"

(Outstanding Achievement Poetry Award Certificates)

7 Golden Poet Award Certificates — World of Poetry

4 Fourth Place Award Certificates and Anthologies — World of Poetry

19 Honorable Mention Award Certificates — World of Poetry

Honorable Mention Award Certificate — Iliad Press

"Longfellow Award" (The National Author's Registry)

Award of Recognition Certificate — Famous Poet for 1996, Famous Poets Society

Honorable Mention Certificate, Spring 1996 — Iliad Press (The National Author's Registry)